SUFFOLK CHURCHES

SUFFOLK CHURCHES

David Stanford

FRANCES LINCOLN

To my wife Jenny,
for all her help, support
and encouragement.

Frances Lincoln Ltd
4 Torriano Mews
Torriano Aveune
London NW5 2RZ
www.franceslincoln.com

Suffolk Churches
Copyright © Frances Lincoln Ltd
2005
Text and photographs copyright ©
David Stanford

First Frances Lincoln edition 2005

A catalogue record for this book is
available from the British Library

ISBN 0 7112 2496 X

Printed and bound in Singapore

9 8 7 6 5 4 3 2 1

Previous page: the nave and
chancel, St Edmund Southwold

CONTENTS

St Peter Monk Soham

INTRODUCTION

All the photographs in this book have been taken digitally. This may be of no consequence to anyone who isn't interested in photography, but for me it was a particularly important reason for the enthusiasm with which I undertook the project. My conventional film cameras now lie unused in their cases. I discarded them some time ago and in the last few years I have undertaken photographic assignments in places as diverse as Ethiopia, Peru and Australia, all with digital cameras. To be truthful, in the early days I had doubts and to be safe always covered things both on film and digitally, but when the results were compared I eventually gave up the use of film. Far from being a threat to the principles of traditional photography, I find this new method of making images truly exciting. As another way of recording what we see as an adjunct to what we feel, it introduces all manner of new experiences to the world of visual interpretation. Digital photography is ridiculed by purists in much the same way as early photographers were ridiculed by painters and engravers, as if what they did was some kind of 'cheating'. But I believe that, as with painting, the only important thing is the final image. How it is achieved is only ever of passing interest. Aesthetic value, if my work can claim any, is too subjective a matter for me to comment on – no doubt others will find no problem doing so – but what can be objectively judged by anyone is whether the quality of these images loses anything in the method used to make them.

Why Suffolk? And why churches? Suffolk is a county that, due to the wealth that wool brought in the Middle Ages, has nearly 700 churches, many of which are extraordinarily beautiful and built in incredibly romantic settings. Why these particular churches? This is a far harder question to answer. This is a completely personal selection. In the course of my travels around the county I have photographed and researched many more churches than are included in this book. Each of the churches in this selection, for one reason or another, commanded my attention or simply stayed in my memory long after I had returned home. Something about each one, not always an architectural or historical feature, caught my always eager eye and fired my imagination.

When I attended Art School in Walthamstow in Essex, I made frequent painting and sketching forays into Suffolk, so I thought I knew the county reasonably well. I foolishly imagined that I was already completely *au fait* with everything it had to offer. But, in the course of gathering material for this book, I travelled much deeper into Suffolk, often getting myself completely lost, discovering that the county is not just beautiful but also very varied. From the rugged sweeping coastline of its North Sea edges to the mysterious and haunting wild woodlands and commons, through the charming and gloriously peaceful historic wool villages, this is a place of fascination. And the parish churches seem to fit into their varied environments with grace and dignity. Suffolk is a place one feels one knows, but do we ever really get to know it completely? With each visit one simply falls further under a spell, and the churches are the very soul of that spell.

Since leaving the Royal College of Art, most of my professional life has been spent in the fields of advertising, fashion and beauty photography. To many of my professional associates, my passion, albeit that of a novice, for history and churches, which stretches back to my early days long before Art School, is something they know nothing about or, if they do, view as one of my many eccentricities. So when Frances Lincoln suggested I compile a book on Suffolk churches, some of them were inevitably surprised. I cannot claim a tremendous amount of scholarship on the subject, so perhaps this is a book about finding out. Like that infamous madeleine, it offers a mere sample tasting and, for some, it might perhaps act as a jog to memories of long ago. If it encourages others to visit or revisit some of the magical places my journey took me, it will have served a purpose. For the enthusiast, it should be a starting point from which to go and make further observations and new discoveries. You will soon realise that I have barely scratched the surface of all that Suffolk churches have to offer.

David Stanford

KEY

Ashby L2
Barsham K3
Beyton E6
Blundeston M2
Bramfield K5
Bures E10
Cavendish D9
Chevington C7

Cockfield E8
Cowlinge B8
Crowfield H7
Denham C7
Denston C8
East Bergholt G10
Erwarton I10
Euston E4
Flixton J3
Frostenden L4

Gazeley B6
Great Blakenham H8
Great Livermere E5
Great Welnetham D7
Hemingstone H8
Hengrave D6
Herringfleet L2
Ixworth Thorpe E5
Kedington B9
Kelsale K6

Long Melford D9
Lound L2
Mellis G5
Mildenhall B5
Monk Soham I6
Moulton B6
Mutord L3
Onehouse F7
Polstead F10
Ramsholt J9

Rumburgh J4
Rushbrooke E7
Shelley G10
Snape K7
Southwold L5
Stannigfield E7
Stoke by Nayland F10
Sudbourne K7
Swilland I8
Theberton L6

Thornham Parva G5
Troston E5
Tuddenham C5
Uggleshall L4
Wenhaston K5
Whepstead D7
Wordwell D5
Wortham G5

ST MARY ASHBY

This lovely church stands at the end of half a mile of lonely country track, in an idyllic setting with far-reaching views towards the marshes. It does not even have a village of the same name to draw its congregation from. This is a place of solitude and peace, but this peaceful old building holds out an unqualified welcome.

The distinctive western tower is Norman, but there has probably been a church here since well before the Conquest. The upper two-thirds of its height, surmounted by battlements, was apparently remodelled in the fifteenth century, at the same time as the nave and chancel, which are thatched. Rather steep steps lead down through the south door into a pleasantly elongated interior containing an unusual, but badly mutilated Purbeck marble font and a fine thirteenth-century piscina under a deeply moulded trefoil arch with a dropped sedilia alongside it. The nave wall carries two painted consecration crosses.

Charming though the interior is, it is unquestionably the completely natural way that this lovely church fits into its surroundings that makes it a place to remember.

The nave and chancel

The font

St Mary Ashby

HOLY TRINITY BARSHAM

Holy Trinity Barsham

The nave and chancel

The tomb of Sir Thomas Echingham

Curiously described in the Domesday Book as 'half a church', Holy Trinity houses several enigmas. Opinion is divided as to whether the round tower is Saxon or Norman. Beyond doubt is that Holy Trinity stands in a lovely pastoral setting next to a pretty rectory.

The chancel was rebuilt, probably using old materials, by Stuart Fleming, a rector here, in 1633. It contains a very fine sixteenth-century tomb, one of only seven Italianate terracotta tombs in East Anglia. On the floor in front of it is a fine, almost intact four-foot brass depicting a knight in full armour. This is identified as Sir Robert atte Tighe, who died in the year of Agincourt, 1415, but it is more likely to be Sir Thomas Echingham, the Royal Seneschal, who succeeded to the Lordship of the Manor in 1450 and who died in 1527. The tomb carries the shield of the Echingham family and this shield has on it the same pattern as another puzzle this church has to offer: the unusual design of the chancel's east wall and window. The entire east wall, including the window, is covered in a bold lattice of strips set in flushwork forming the lozenge-shaped tracery of the window itself. Once thought medieval, this rarity is now considered

to be part of the restoration work carried out in the seventeenth century, and it seems very likely that the individuality of his design was inspired by the Echingham coat of arms. It is a striking feature, which now has stained glass designed by Kempe in the 1870s. Twenty-five figures in beautifully subtle colours fill the window, one in each lozenge.

The nave, rethatched after a disastrous fire in 1979, stands slightly higher than the chancel. The simple interior with double-arched arcade to the north provides a warm welcome and much interest: a Stuart pulpit, a partly Jacobean screen and a faded painting of St Christopher plus two fonts: an unused marble Norman font bowl, discovered under the floor, and the fine fifteenth-century one.

Horatio Nelson's grandfather was the parson here in 1714–30 and Nelson's mother was born in the rectory. In 1905, to commemorate the centenary of the battle of Trafalgar, the central nave window was designed with the garlanded shields and roundels of several generations of the Suckling family, the ancestors of England's great naval hero.

ALL SAINTS BEYTON

Beyton, originally on the main road between Cambridge and the sea, would have been very familiar to the Puritan William Dowsing as he journeyed relentlessly backwards and forwards on his destructive jaunts in the 1640s. He did visit All Saints and he did destroy items, but mercifully not on his usual vindictive scale.

The heavily buttressed round tower, which may be Norman or Saxon, stands resolute and fortress-like. When viewed from a slight angle at the gate, the handsome tower amply hides the quite hideous modern vestry to the south, giving some indication of how the imposing structure of the original building would have appeared for centuries before that sad addition. Enter through the unimposing porch, however, and you find a nave that is almost totally Victorianised. There is little that is outstanding here apart from some nice nineteenth-century bench ends with carved backs and traditional poppyheads mixed with animals, in particular a charming unicorn. A stained glass window depicts the parable of the sower (Matthew 13: 13) and other pleasant details to give a calm and natural quality. The highlight of this generally unprepossessing interior is undoubtedly the reredos depicting the Last Supper. The eye is drawn to this from the far end of the nave, demanding closer inspection.

For me, however, it is undoubtedly the exterior of this fine building that makes it worth visiting.

All Saints Beyton

ST MARY BLUNDESTON

St Mary Blundeston

The church at 'Blunderstone' is mentioned at the beginning of Charles Dickens' *David Copperfield*, although it has greatly changed since Dickens' time and the distracting memorial to 'Mr Bodgers, late of this Parish' is nowhere to be found and probably never existed. However it is a fitting location for that wonderful story.

Set in a wild, flat churchyard two miles from the sea and the River Waveney, this is an ancient building, mentioned in the Anglo Saxon Chronicles of 666. The tall, tapering round tower, which is said to have been built in 988, has four blocked Saxon round belfry windows beneath four thirteenth-century lancet windows, added when the structure was heightened and battlements added to crown it. The church itself is not aligned with the tower due to the widening of the traditionally narrow earlier building, probably to accommodate a growing congregation. Inside the tower an arch opens into the nave, which was rebuilt in the fourteenth century. The pleasant interior contains a lovely, primitive dado decorated with painted angels, a twelfth-century octagonal font, some seventeenth-century brasses and a fine trefoiled sedilia. One rather strange object, above the door, is a coat of arms of Charles II dated 1673. The heraldry is curiously inaccurate, indicating that this is probably an over-painting of an earlier hatchment. Until the nineteenth century, these Royal Arms would, by law, have occupied the space in the chancel arch. Were the discrepancies not noticed when it was moved to its present position or was it left to be corrected later then the correcting forgotten?

The nave and chancel

The dado

Here is a Norman round tower with a difference. It is completely detached and separate from the church. It has been argued that all round towers were originally built like this, the churches only being attached later. However, this is the only round tower in England that can actually be proven never to have been attached to its church.

This lovely, unusual church is approached through a lychgate directly opposite the serpentine wall of Bramfield Hall. It is largely fourteenth-century, with a thatched nave and chancel and a very modest porch. The building was sympathetically restored in the 1870s with little loss to its main features, so Bramfield can thankfully still boast the finest rood screen in East Anglia. It dates to the early sixteenth century and is largely unrestored, a little faded but magnificent. The carving and colour are simply gorgeous. Although only five of the dado panels depicting saints and evangelists remain, it is an inspiring piece, in which art meets craftsmanship to perfection.

A very welcoming interior holds much to admire, particularly a fine monument created by Nicholas Stone in 1629 in memory of Arthur Coke and his wife Elizabeth. She died in childbirth in 1627 and he survived her by just a few years. Life-sized, he kneels in armour, praying despairingly under a sombre black arch edged with heraldry, while below him his wife lies on a bed tragically cradling their baby daughter. Mounted high on the wall on either side of the monument are two breastplates and helmets of a slightly earlier period.

The Rabett family, who lived at Bramfield Hall for three hundred years, are also well represented by their various hatchments hanging on the walls. The family coat of arms makes ample use of rabbits, a pun on their name. The font is fourteenth-century and, in a recess on the north wall of the nave, there is what remains of a wall painting.

It is a puzzle how so much of this church and its treasures managed to survive the attentions of Dowsing and other destructive religious bigots down the centuries. We can only be thankful that it did.

The rood screen

Two of the dado panels

The monument to Arthur Coke and his wife

ST ANDREW BRAMFIELD

St Andrew Bramfield

ST STEPHEN BURES

St Stephen Bures

The nave

Here at Bures we are on the edge of Suffolk, where the county line drifts languorously, giving little indication as to whether you are in Suffolk or Essex. Bures has a lovely parish church of its own, but this strange chapel is something of an oddity. Finding St Stephen takes some determination, but perseverance is richly rewarded. A key can be obtained from a very friendly local farmer, then a brisk walk across lovely sweeping countryside ends with what looks like a large, thatched roofed barn – and this is exactly what it was for a great many years. Why such a chapel should exist here in the middle of nowhere is something of a mystery. Some claim that this is the spot where St Edmund was crowned king of East Anglia in 855, a fact that is almost impossible to substantiate. However, it is known that this rustic building was consecrated by Bishop Stephen Langton in 1218 and there must have been some important reason for this.

Inside the chapel lies a surprise: three fine monuments representing two knights with crossed legs and a lady with an elaborate head-dress and puppies at her feet. These are the de Veres, Earls of Oxford. The tombs were moved here from Earls Colne Priory, the family burial place, and almost certainly what one sees now are reconstructions using various parts from a number of other original de Vere tombs from the priory. Pevsner believed that the main tomb chest did not belong and was more likely to have been a shrine that was reused. That being said, the quality of the carving is fine, and the actual effigy figures have not suffered as much mutilation as they might have in a less remote setting. Lancet windows contain some lovely fragments of stained glass that also came from the priory as well the bottom half of a twelfth-century carved coffin lid which is probably that of Alberic, 1st Earl of Oxford and Great Chamberlain, who died in 1141.

This chapel is a puzzle. Why did it have such an impressive consecration, and why are the tombs of such an exalted family in what could pass for a large farm building?

ST MARY CAVENDISH

The word 'quaint' seems almost derogatory, but the fact is that Cavendish is quaint, and beautiful for that. The lovely church stands proudly in a churchyard studded with mature trees on the north side of a wide village green circled by medieval cottages, testifying to the wealth of this area during the Middle Ages. A great deal of this wealth was lavished on the churches of the area, mostly to the glory of God, sometimes in a blatant attempt to secure a place in Heaven and often as a status symbol.

A Saxon church stood here, followed by a Norman one, but the present building dates mainly from *c.*1300, when the tower was built. In 1425 a north aisle was added, and a clerestory in 1485. The tower boasts a massive south-east stair turret, which rises well above the battlements giving access to what were once the living quarters of the priest. At the top of this internal staircase is a room with a fireplace, complete with a hidden chimney and a small window that gave the incumbent a clear view of the altar. Fifty years later the south aisle walls were rebuilt with windows, probably to the design of Reginald Ely, Henry VI's architect, whose claim to fame was that he began the magnificent King's College Chapel in Cambridge. In 1381 Sir John Cavendish, the Lord Chief Justice of the King's Bench, bequeathed forty pounds for the construction of a chancel. Unfortunately the poor man reaped little benefit from this generosity since, during the peasants revolt, he was dragged out and beheaded by the locals in revenge for the part his son played in the death of Wat Tyler, the peasant leader.

Like many of the grander churches of Suffolk, Cavendish boasts a tall, wide nave, flooded with light not only from the clerestory but from the mass of glass at the east end of the church. In addition to the many fine architectural merits of the interior there are numerous fascinating objects to be seen, such as the tomb, in the sanctuary, of Sir John Colt of Colt Hall, who died in 1570. Strangely, the top of this tomb has a board clearly scratched on it for playing the game 'Alquerque', a form of Nine Men's Morris. However, the gem in the crown of this church has to be the superb and very rare sixteenth-century Flemish rederos, with its extraordinarily fine bas-relief crucifixion scene in painted alabaster.

The unusually low fourteenth-century south porch has a door with a sanctuary ring, which still retains the rivets that possibly once carried carved metal lizards (symbolic of good fortune). Outside the porch, to the right, is a scratch dial or mass clock, used in the past by villagers to judge the time for services at a glance.

Many tourists visit Cavendish, but to miss seeing the church is to have bypassed the ageless heart of this lovely village.

Above: St Mary Cavendish
Below left: The reredos
Below middle: The tomb of Sir John Colt
Below right: The east window

The tie beam roof

The nave and chancel

The carved bench ends

This church has a long and chequered history. Abbot Baldwin acquired the manor in the mid-eleventh century and it remained under the control of the Benedictine Abbey of Bury St Edmunds up until the dissolution of the monasteries in 1539. The manor was then granted to Thomas Kytson of Hengrave, eventually being sold on to the Earls of Bristol in 1716. It remains part of the Marquess of Bristol's estates.

There was certainly a church here, probably wooden, before the Norman Conquest, and that building served the community for many years before being replaced by a stone building around 1130. Evidence of the Norman stone structure is still to be seen in the nave, but some time in the thirteenth century the east end of the church was extended by twenty feet to form a chancel. This, however, was shortened again in 1697 due to subsidence and a simple, lovely east window was added. The present church is a large building, with something of the look of a folly about it. Money had been left in 1480 to build a sturdy west tower in the Perpendicular style. In 1817 the 4th Earl of Bristol, Bishop of Derry, heightened it, adding picturesque crocketed pinnacles, apparently for no other reason than to give a more bucolic view from his grand house, Ickworth Park, near by.

The porch is largely a reconstruction, but its striking original entrance arch is fourteenth-century, formed from two huge curved timbers skilfully cut from one massive piece of wood by medieval carpenters to exactly mirror one another.

The interior is outstanding in its simplicity. White light pervades and the unusual use of space and shape soaks it up. Lofty tie beams, inscribed with the dates 1590 and 1638 and the initials of churchwardens, brace the structure. The wonderful tall, narrow chancel arch is flanked on each side by smaller, complimentary arches which give further views of one of the most beautifully simple chancels and modern altars to be seen anywhere in the country.

An early coat of arms of George I hangs high above the entrance and a marvellous medieval chest with intricate decoration stands opposite. Among a host of fifteenth-century carved bench end figures are musicians playing all manner of instruments, including lutes, cymbals and bagpipes. Interestingly, these musical references may have been conceived under the influence of John Wilbye, the greatest composer of madrigals in the period 1595–1630. He was the Kytsons' and then the Gales' household musician. Since those families owned this manor and visited it frequently from their seat at Hengrave, it is very likely he accompanied them. One can only imagine what musical treats he devised for the congregation.

All Saints Chevington is a little known church full of quiet simplicity and complete individuality, a place of both past and present worship.

ALL SAINTS CHEVINGTON

All Saints Chevington

ST PETER COCKFIELD

St Peter Cockfield

This attractively imposing building is built in a mixture of flint, herringbone redbrick and timber and enriched with elaborate battlements on the tower, aisles and porch. The early fourteenth-century chancel, with a priest's door and startling devil gargoyles, is seamlessly joined to a nave capped with a five-light clerestory, which in turn merges with the strong west tower. In the eighteenth century, one of the rectors, an enthusiastic astronomer, had uncharacteristic windows cut under the parapets on the north and south walls of the tower to accommodate his telescope. The south aisle meets a fine porch built in the 1460s and, to complete the balance, lovely Perpendicular style windows run the whole length of the building.

Just inside the porch are three deep niches that once held statues, with fleurons and shields above the arch of the doorway. Inside, the fifteenth-century tie beam roof, which until 1879 was coloured, has unusual king posts that are braced four ways. The five bay arcades have octagonal piers. The windows in the south aisle have remains of some good fourteenth-century glass. The north aisle, now the vestry, was once a chapel with a room above it. On the north wall of the chancel is a fine monument with a central black sarcophagus supporting the wigless bust of James Harvey, who died of smallpox in Cambridge in 1722. South of the altar there is a fifteenth-century panel of glass depicting St Anne teaching the Virgin Mary to read. In the nave a seventeenth-century pulpit stands on an earlier carved pedestal and at the other end of the church is a plain fourteenth-century font.

The monument to James Harvey

One of the south windows

ST MARGARET OF ANTIOCH COWLINGE

Visiting this sturdy, exotically dedicated and seemingly remote church, it is hard to believe that you are only a few miles from the busy A143. It stands on raised ground north of the village. The medieval part of the church is built of brick and septaria but the builders almost certainly used material from an earlier church. In the eighteenth century, the heavy buttresses were added to support a bowing chancel, giving the building a powerful footprint, and the stark redbrick Georgian tower was built. However, very little Victorian restoration work was done and the building has retained a rustic eccentricity, both externally and internally. Entering the fifteenth-century north porch one is presented with an ancient door, the piers and arch of which are covered with fascinating graffiti from many different periods throughout the building's changing history.

The chancel is wider than the nave and not aligned to it, and these proportions owe something to the fact that, traditionally, the care and upkeep of the chancel were the remit of the rector, but the upkeep of the nave was the responsibility of the parishioners. Light floods through the clerestory windows, and a preliminary appraisal takes the eye along the lofty nave to a massive tie beam crown post, which dominates part of the roof space. Above a beautifully carved screen, one of only two in the county to retain its original doors, is the haughty chancel arch which exhibits one of the wonders this church has to offer, the remains of a large painting. But this is not a traditional doom painting. To the right of the arch is a representation of St Michael with a set of scales, weighing the soul of a sinner, while to the left the Virgin Mary reaches out with a wand and tips the balance in favour of the sinner. Such blatant iconography would have been total anathema to sixteenth-century reformers but luckily this fascinating example was saved from complete destruction by being whitewashed over. The painting was rediscovered during extensive refurbishment in 1914, only months before the First World War was to drastically reduce the populations of so many of these villages.

At the west end of the north aisle are four uncomfortable, backless wooden forms, set in tiers, in the coldest part of the church. We are informed that these were installed, by special permission, in 1618 to accommodate the keeper of Cowlinge House of Correction and his prisoners. Dominating the chancel is an amusingly ostentatious monument to Francis Dickin (died 1747). Clad in Roman togas he and his wife cast down an imperial glare. In the western gallery under the Dickin's coat of arms a Latin inscription translates, in a parody of the Emperor Augustus describing his contribution to the building of Rome, that 'he found the roof of this temple made of straw . . . and he left it made of brick and he built it with one tower only'. Indeed he did build the tower and carry out other extensive restoration work in his time, but he surely suffered from delusions of grandeur. This is a simple village church, hardly the Roman senate. An interesting point about this proud memorial is that it is the only example of the work of Peter Sheemaker in Suffolk. Sheemaker also gave us the bust of Shakespeare in Westminster Abbey. The bust represents Sheemaker's own notion of how the Bard looked rather than any known likeness. Was he a specialist in personal fantasy?

St Margaret of Antioch Cowlinge

ALL SAINTS CROWFIELD

All Saints Crowfield

The timber chancel

The chancel interior

Until 1920 All Saints was not even regarded as a church, but was known as Crowfield Chapel. This is not surprising since it is a long way from the village, totally hidden from the road and, if not a complete secret, at least a wonderful surprise.

Approached from the east through what used to be the grounds of an old manor house, this unique Suffolk religious building is reached by a small gate. We find what appears to be a simple fourteenth-century nave, but with a wonderful fifteenth-century timber chancel attached. There is simply no other church building remotely like this in the county. It resembles nothing so much as a medieval church converted into a Tudor farmhouse, then, after second thoughts, changed back to a place of worship. While a few buildings of a similar look to this exist in the north of England, how did this quirky and loveable building find its way here?

Visitors are presented with a delight of building styles from a number of different periods. The body of the building appears to consist of traditional fourteenth-century stonework with not entirely unexpected Perpendicular windows. Unusually, they have timber-framed mullions and tracery. A curiously positioned bell turret, which replaces an earlier cupola, sits jauntily, not as one would expect over the western gable, but just off-centre along the nave roof.

The church is set in a spacious and tranquil churchyard, its solitary position adding further to the fairytale ambience. One enters through a magical fifteenth-century south porch, which delights in displaying the talents of the carpenters who created it. The interior has undergone its fair share of Victorian 'improvements', which included the removal of what must have been very interesting box pews (a common dislike of Victorian renovators). Fortunately, the beautiful timber framework of the chancel remains intact (this chancel was originally completely timber) and no amount of restoration can rob it of the character it still lends the place. There is also a late fifteenth-century hammerbeam roof in the nave, below which are slight traces of the fixtures of a rood screen. This is also sadly long gone, but local tradition claims it was a very fine one. Before leaving, look out for the two ancient stone carvings: one of a grotesque human head, the other of an animal head. There could be no more fitting fantastical decoration for a place of enchantment as this.

Due to its remote position the church is understandably kept locked, but the key can be obtained from a very kind lady at No. 1 Church Road, a mile or so back in the village.

The tomb of Sir Edward and Lady Susan Lewkenor

The kneeling tomb figures

The table tomb of Sir Edward Lewkenor

There are two Denhams in Suffolk. The other is near Eye.

St Mary lies between Bury St Edmunds and Newmarket. It is a little remote and very easily missed since it lies up a very small lane off a small road south-west of Barrow. At first glance the church might make you wonder why you had gone to all the effort to get there, but any initial disappointment is soon dispelled. It is true that the church itself in unimposing. Almost all of it is nineteenth-century with a blocked Norman door giving the only hint of its early origins. Closer inspection reveals a peculiar appendage to the north of the chancel – a large seventeenth-century redbrick extension. It is this that you have come to see.

It is only upon entering the largely Victorianised interior that it becomes apparent that the addition is in fact a mortuary chapel. The chapel is separated from the chancel by three plain arches and on the far wall there is a very unusual and massive monument. Six Corinthian columns hold aloft an elaborate canopy bearing a full heraldic achievement beneath which are ten almost life-sized figures. This is the tomb of Sir Edward and Lady Susan Lewkenor, who died of smallpox within days of each other in 1605. Still retaining much of their original colouring, Sir Edward and his wife kneel, he in armour, she in a black head-dress. Behind them are their eight children in two columns, two sons to the fore and six daughters behind. The figures may be primitive and clumsily executed, but they are undoubtedly historically intriguing and not easily ignored.

On an adjacent wall is the far-from-primitive table tomb of their grandson, another Sir Edward. The last of the line, he also died of smallpox, in 1635. This finely crafted work, in alabaster and marble, was carried out by the favourite craftsmen of Charles I, John and Matthias Christmas. Sir Edward lies with his hand on his heart in the full armour and characteristic lace collar of the Civil War he would miss, a slightly disappointed look on his aristocratic face.

ST MARY DENHAM

St Mary Denham

ST NICHOLAS DENSTON

St Nicholas Denston

The carved roof timbers

For a fairly remote village with, even today, only 137 inhabitants, this is a very grand church. Considered by many to be Suffolk's finest small church, it has close connections with Holy Trinity Long Melford and may even have been designed by the same architect. In 1475, in accordance with the will of John Denston, whose wife Katherine was a Clopton of Long Melford, a chantry college with three priests was founded. This lasted less than a hundred years. In 1547 all its assets were seized by the Crown.

All but the tower of this church was built during the 1460s. The nave, chancel, clerestory, aisles and chapels are all late Perpendicular in style and almost overpower the earlier short, heavily butressed, fourteenth-century tower. The south porch has beautiful fan vaulting and fifteenth-century double doors. Once the scale and layout of the interior, with its tall seven-bay arcade and great number of windows, has been noted, it is the wealth of carving that catches the eye. It is everywhere. The unusually pale timbers of the roof are covered with carved foliage, lions, dogs and wonderfully agile hares. There are box pews and benches displaying further skilful carvings. In all, sixty creatures appear, among them a very peculiar elephant, foxes, a goose and a unicorn. A remnant of the old college is to be seen in the lovely stalls, four of which still retain their misericords, one showing a rare and beautifully carved crane from the medieval bestiary.

The marble-topped tomb

Between the high altar and the north chapel is a marble-topped tomb that, while not strictly speaking a cadaver tomb, has two rather frightening figures in shrouds lying underneath it. The woman's shroud is strangely tied at the head, while the man's is torn open to reveal his skeletal chest, a gruesome reminder of the medieval preoccupation with death. Since the descriptive brasses are missing it is not known who they are, but it is likely they are the same John and Katherine Denston responsible for bequeathing the college and whose portraits appear in the stained glass at Long Melford.

At the centre of the chancel there are also two important brasses with 26-inch figures. These are Henry Everard (died 1524) and his wife Margaret. They are the only heraldic pair on separate brasses in Suffolk. Henry wears a heraldic tabard over armour and helmet, while his wife has a head-dress of the period and a heraldic mantle displaying the arms of her husband and her father. During the reign of Elizabeth I, the manor passed to the Robinson family and high on the wall of the south chapel hangs a splendid helm with a golden stag crest, a sword and a tabard with the Robinson arms.

It is hard to believe that in 1948 the state of this church was described as desolate and decayed with rats gnawing at everything. It is far from that now.

The carved bench ends

The nave and chancel

The arms of the Cardinall family

East Bergholt is in the heart of Constable country and this church looks like it could be an enormous romantic folly set in one of his exquisite landscapes. Indeed, he did many early studies of St Mary, the church in which he was baptised and where his parents are buried. As a young man Constable paid court to the incumbent's grand-daughter Maria Bicknell, much to the pompous reverend's horror and opposition, but after seven years Constable was finally allowed to marry her. Also connected with East Bergholt are the de Vere Earls of Oxford, Lords of the Manor from Norman times. Edward, the 17th Earl (whom some scholars credit with the works of Shakespeare), finally sold the family holdings off in 1578. With historical associations like these, coaches and tourists are always to be found here. Nevertheless they should not detract from the special features of a great wool church that never quite reached its final statement.

Competition between villages must have sparked the building of the tower since the impressive walk-through tower at nearby Dedham would have been a challenge to the upwardly mobile inhabitants of East Bergholt. Work on their own tower commenced in 1525 and tradition tells that it was made possible thanks to promised funds from Cardinal Wolsey. Alas, Wolsey fell from grace after building commenced and his funds ended up in Henry VIII's bottomless pocket. This tale is probably apocryphal; it is far more likely that the local wool-wealthy family (coincidentally named Cardinall) promised funds but due to the Reformation and growing Protestant sympathy in the village the tower just never got finished. The outcome of this was, however, another peculiarity: the bell cage, which was built in 1531 to house the bells as a temporary measure. Other bell cages exist, but at East Berholt the bells are rung by force of hand, and that makes it unique, especially when one considers that they are the heaviest set of bells still to be rung in England.

Nothing remains of the church that is earlier than the fourteenth century, since it was largely rebuilt in the fifteenth and early sixteenth centuries but inside and out there many delightful details, for example, the peculiar sight of a camel and a bear on the north wall. They are part of a tomb that would have been originally in the north chapel but was clumsily moved to accommodate the Victorian organ. The animals depicted are the heraldic devices of the Cardinall family and this was part of a monument to Anne Parker, the heiress of that family. An Easter sepulchre painting that must have been very impressive is also in evidence, as are some touching inscriptions such as this: 'Here till the sun of glory rise/My dearest darke and dusty lies.' Shades of Shakespeare (or is it Edward de Vere)?

All these treasures and many more lie in an interior bathed in light from the ten-window clerestory. What a treasure trove this church is to visit.

ST MARY EAST BERGHOLT

St Mary East Bergholt

ST MARY THE VIRGIN ERWARTON

St Mary the Virgin Erwarton

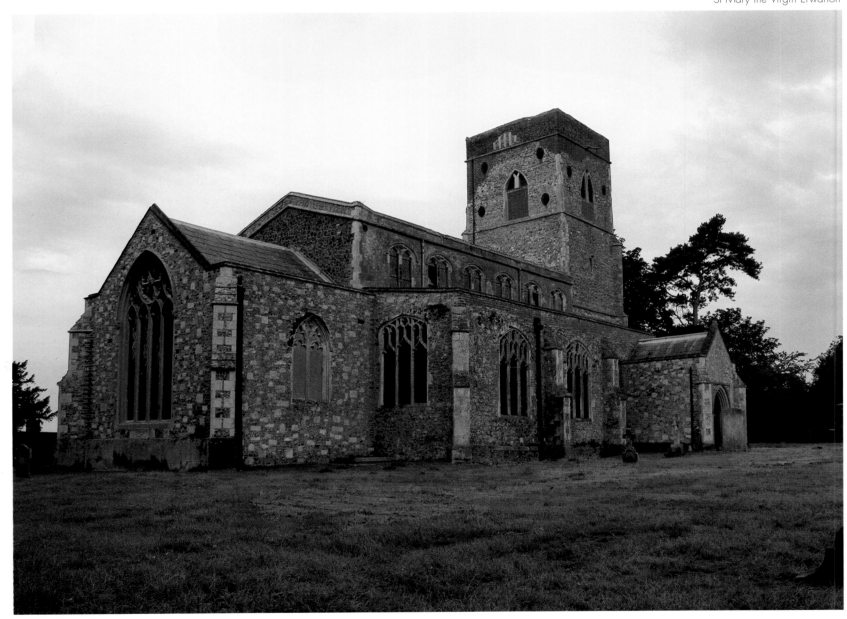

Although much altered over the years and only hinting at its former glory, this spacious church, constructed with characteristic local septaria stone, mostly in the Perpendicular style, makes a forceful statement. Standing in a churchyard backed by a view of the estuary of the River Stour, this is an imposing building. The approach road runs past the lovely old manor house of Erwarton Hall with its spectacular Tudor gatehouse. Church and house have an inextricably intertwined history reaching across the centuries and it is the visual testament to this that makes the church so interesting.

The interior of the present church is largely the result of a fifteenth-century rebuild but some of the tombs are much older, and provide a historic role-call of the families who have owned the manor during its long history: the d'Avilliers (c.1200–1300), the Bacons (1330–81), the Calthorpes (1381–1549) and the Parkers (1549–1741). Although moved many times, these tombs constitute a unique genealogical record. On the south wall lies a cross-legged Crusader knight, probably Sir Bartholomew d'Avilliers, who died in 1287. Further along lies a tomb with the effigies of Sir Bartholomew Bacon and his wife, who died in 1391 and 1435 respectively. Sir Bartholomew lies with his head of long wavy hair resting on a massive helm next to his wife Anne, who wears a beautifully detailed crespine (the net head-dress fashionable in the period). Both figures are finely carved and retain traces of their original bright colouring. On the opposite wall a canopy flanked by pinnacles holds an effigy of a small woman wearing a wimple. This is thought to be Isabel d'Avilliers, who married Robert Bacon in c.1330.

There are numerous other memorials and brasses from various periods hidden away throughout the church, but it is to the Parkers that interest ultimately turns. The Parkers were close relatives of Anne Boleyn through her aunt, Armata, and it is known that as a child Anne often visited the manor. There are, of course, countless legends associated with Anne Boleyn but this one has something of a twist. The story goes that the ill-fated queen often expressed the wish to have her heart buried at Erwarton, the scene of much childhood happiness, and that after her execution the Parkers carried out her wish. The story joined the host of other apocryphal Boleyn legends until, in 1836, during building work, a small heart-shaped casket was found in a wall. It contained only dust. It was resealed, placed on a coffin in the vault and reburied. Coincidence? Whatever your view this is a lovely and historic place.

The tomb of Sir Bartholomew d'Avilliers

The tomb of Sir Bartholomew Bacon and his wife Anne

Stained glass

The nave

Stained glass

To judge from appearances alone you could be forgiven for thinking that you were in London looking at something by Wren or an associate. This is a seventeenth-century Anglican country church, one of only a handful remodelled or rebuilt in 1670s rural England, and unique in Suffolk. It stands in a vast country estate, from which the original village was moved to accommodate the grand house and parkland. The estate was acquired for a song by Lord Arlington in the 1660s from the previous owners, the Rokewodes, a Catholic family ruined by their association with the Gunpowder Plot. The acquisition was undoubtedly endorsed by the Crown as a reward to Lord Arlington for his staunch support of the Royalist cause. The estate soon passed from Lord Arlington to Henry Fitzroy 1st Duke of Grafton, the illegitimate son of Charles II, by marriage to Arlington's only child Isabella. There are ten Dukes of Grafton buried in the vaults.

Closer inspection reveals that, far from being a pure Restoration work, most of its outer walls are those of a medieval church. Little is known of the original building but when Lord Arlington took over the estate it was in dire condition and money for work was granted by the Bishop of Norwich as early as 1671, through to completion in 1676. However, only the south aisle seems to have been totally rebuilt. On its outer wall, next to an unused south door, a stone inscription states that 'The Duches of Grafton and Countese of Ewston layed this stone 21st day of April 1676'. This was Isabella, who was only eight years old when she became engaged to Henry Fitzroy.

The finished result appeared like a completely new building. The tower was heightened at this time and opulence, grace and harmony governed the overall design inside and out. No one knows who the architect was but various influences are recognisable. The interior is a truly elegant statement, with a wonderful pulpit that was unfortunately moved from its original position to halfway down the nave, depriving it of its fine sounding board. Fine box pews and panelling, alongside various ornate carved memorials, add to the post-Restoration flavour of the interior. However, brasses commemorating the original owners date back as far as 1480 and there is stained glass from the Victorian era, making this building quite a *feste* of the history of style.

The bucolic churchyard and the observatory on the hill behind the church augment the whole, but you will have to collect the key from the Estate Office if you want to see inside this beautifully idiosyncratic church.

ST GENEVIEVE EUSTON

St Genevieve Euston

St Mary Flixton

ST MARY FLIXTON

The statue of Lady Theodosia Waveney

Records show that a church was first built here in *c.*700 and in Saxon times a stone church with a tower was constructed. But the principal interest in the present church lies in the controversy that stems from its tower and its similarity to one at Sompting in Sussex. Some believe that the very unusual tower at Flixton is an accurate copy of the ancient original that collapsed in 1835. Others believe that the tower is simply a Victorian creation. This is far from a dry pointless argument, as the ancient church at Sompting is the only one of its kind in the British Isles. If the tower at Flixton is a copy of the original it places this church in the ranks of historically important ecclesiastic buildings. The debate is fierce and even Pevsner refuses to commit himself categorically to one side or the other.

What is known is that the Victorian architect Anthony Salvin did an enthusiastically thorough job of rebuilding the church in 1861, so there is very little left of the original building, which had steadily fallen into disrepair after the Black Death in 1349. Some thirteenth-century pillars, a fourteenth-century four-bay north arcade along with some bench ends that appear to be medieval are really all that survived his attention. However, if you enjoy the Victorian period, it is further represented by the Waveney Chapel, with its columned and fan-vaulted roof, housing a marble statue of Lady Theodosia Waveney by John Bell.

A pre-1835 drawing or painting of the church could put the tower controversy to rest, and one may yet appear. Until then, visit and choose your camp.

ALL SAINTS FROSTENDEN

All Saints Frostenden

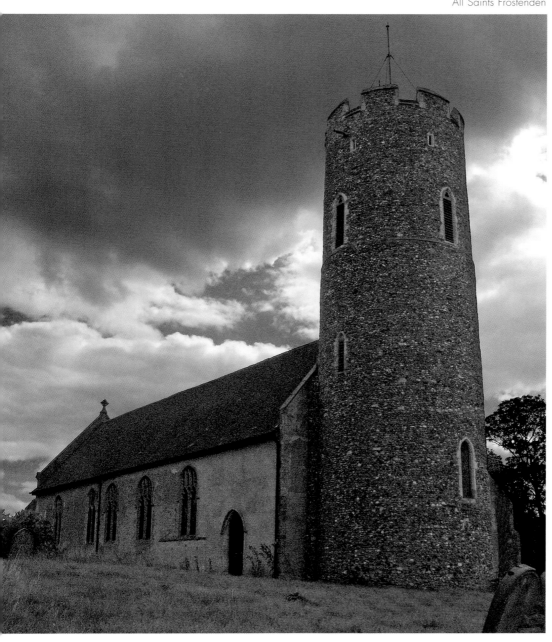

It is hard to imagine that this lonely place was, at the time of the Norman Conquest, a seaport with a well established community. The church now stands commandingly on raised ground but with only a farm for company. This is one of Suffolk's earliest round tower churches, undoubtedly Saxon in origin. In view of its former seaward position (the sea and river have long retreated many miles away) it is likely that this tower also served a defensive role. Robustly constructed largely of coarse whole flints, the tower puts forward a strong defiant stance while offering some architectural rarities. These include a small dressed stone alcove for a statue low down on the tower wall and two quern stones (for grinding corn) that have been integrated into the lower stonework. Was this merely to make use of some spare stone or did this make some other symbolic statement? The question remains unanswered.

The body of the church is mainly thirteenth-century with a fine fourteenth-century porch complete with a delightful carving of a pelican on its centre boss. Externally and internally there is a wealth of other fascinating carving – animals, humans and grotesques – waiting for the curious eye to discover. Another interesting feature is the pretty old sundial above the entrance, which demands that we watch and pray ('Vigilate et Orate'). An interesting and well kept interior is reached through a medieval door of lapped boards, but it is the really the sheer external presence of the building as whole which is the major wonder of this church.

ALL SAINTS GAZELEY

All Saints Gazeley

Standing in a large churchyard on raised ground, this church could not wish for a better position for passers-by to admire it, but it seems lonely and neglected. It is difficult to gain entrance and the exterior has clearly suffered some mindless vandalism. Yet there is so much to be applauded about the building.

From the outside alone the uniqueness of this mainly thirteenth-century church soon becomes apparent. The east window of the chancel is possibly the most remarkable example of the Decorated style in the whole of Suffolk. Dating from about 1330 it has three tall narrow lights in a most unusual configuration. The chancel itself was completed just as the Black Death began to decimate Europe. Yet even in this period of turmoil the medieval mind was still capable of producing architecture of great beauty. In the sixteenth-century the nave, aisles and clerestory were rebuilt, all with the Perpendicular style windows characteristic of the time.

If you are able to gain entry, you will see, above the chancel, the lovely sixteenth-century wagon roof with its little angels carrying scrolls, ears of wheat and vines, and the clerestory, to which the Victorians decided, unusually, to move valuable medieval stained glass. Although rather defeating the purpose of a clerestory – which is to let in as much light as possible – this may well have saved the glass from the vandalism it might have suffered lower down. High above it is possible to make out two demi-angels, the three crowns of East Anglia, St Faith and St Apollonia, a shield representing the trinity, a bishop with a mitre and three more angels – a beautifully wrought collection.

Also of interest are the fourteenth-century font, the Perpendicular pulpit with arched panels, the interesting benches – some of which may have been constructed from parts of the screen – and a conundrum. On the back of one of the benches appear the words 'Salaman Sayet'. Might this possibly mean 'Solomon Sayeth'?

All this and much more awaits the visitor. Perhaps a steady stream of visitors might awaken the village to the neglected treasure it has in its midst.

ST MARY GREAT BLAKENHAM

The carved porch

Unfortunately, this church has none of the quiet peace it deserves. Although neatly set in a pretty raised churchyard, it fronts on to the main Ipswich to Norwich road in an ugly village that forms part of the great urban sprawl emanating from Ipswich. This is a beautiful church, however, and bears its position with nobility.

The rather plain Norman tower is capped with a fourteenth-century top, the rendering of which unfortunately tends to give it an unsatisfactory concrete look. The classic Norman nave combines well with a rare example of an Early English chancel. Entering through a charming fifteenth-century wooden porch things start to impress. On the front of the central porch support is a delightful early wood carving of the Madonna. Has it been defaced or is its appearance due to the wear and tear of hundreds of years? Dowsing came here in 1644 but his destructive instructions were mild and do not seem to have been carried out with too much enthusiasm. The interior is a true delight. The thick walls, a hallmark of Norman builders, offer an unexpected silence and coolness. To the east, deep and impressively splayed triple lancet windows, with a smaller circular window above, stand over the altar ready to pour in light on the darkest day. There is an octagonal font in the Perpendicular style and a monument, dated 1645, in memory of Richard Swift, celebrating his life and Baltic associations in amusing rhyme. It has now taken on a secondary function as a decorative stand for flowers and other ornaments. This church is a delight, albeit surrounded by modern urban expansion.

St Mary Great Blakenham

ST PETER GREAT LIVERMERE

The nave and chancel

A detail of one of the wall paintings

Hemmed in as it is by modern houses, this is still a lovely church with much individuality. A Norman thatched nave joins the square west tower, which is barely higher than it. The stonework of the tower is topped with a charming wooden pyramid. Some of the chancel windows have been blocked. The ochre colouring of the wash used on the external walls enhances the look of this building.

Entering through the south porch into a light interior, one immediately confronts the wall paintings on the north nave wall. These are fourteenth-century, one probably a St Christopher, due to its position opposite the door, the other, behind the organ, part of a representation of the Three Quick and the Three Dead, a medieval morality story. There are also the remains of some further, much faded, paintings on the nave south wall, including a *Noli Me Tangere*. How the puritan iconoclasts missed something as provocative as this is a mystery. The chancel roof has beautifully carved broad wall plates with various leaf and tracery patterns. Other features worthy of note are the fine, rare three-decker pulpit, dated 1700, and a variety of benches, one dated 1601.

A matter of passing interest is a memorial in the chancel to M.R. James, the famed ghost story writer, whose father was the vicar here. Before leaving through the pleasant churchyard, look just east of the porch for the headstone to William Sakings (died 1689). He was falconer to three successive kings, Charles I, Charles II and James II, a feat of survival considering the troubled times he saw in such a profession.

St Peter Great Livermere

ST THOMAS A BECKET
GREAT WHELNETHAM

The unusual carved symbol

This is a delightful little church, rather like a small country house in appearance. There is some faint evidence of much earlier origins but the chancel with its lancet windows is certainly thirteenth-century. A tiny, unprepossessing clerestory, totally unlike its many grand cousins scattered across the county, adds to the domestic feel of the building. Inside there is an octagonal font in the Perpendicular style, fragments of glass from various periods in the south-east chancel window and a pulpit dating from *c*.1500. A charming weatherboard bell turret, dated 1749 according to Pevsner, is placed over the nave. A proper tower probably never existed. The dedication to Thomas à Becket is an interesting survival in view of the fact that after 1530 most references to him or imagery regarding his story were destroyed or removed.

Before leaving, note of the unusual symbol embedded into the external fabric of the building, at the eastern end of the south wall of the nave.

St Thomas à Becket Great Whelnetham

ST GREGORY HEMINGSTONE

St Gregory Hemingstone

The monument to William Cantrell

The nave

Hemingstone (or Haminghelanda) carries a lengthy entry in the Domesday Book. Perhaps it was a large and active settlement then, but certainly not now. Remote and not really on the route to anywhere, its only near neighbours are a sixteenth-century farm and an odd village hall, but a visit will be rewarded.

The church stands in an idyllic position on an ancient raised site. This is one of only thirteen churches in Suffolk that show indisputable evidence of a pre-1066 building. The Saxon long-and-short stonework at the south-west corner of the nave firmly dates the first rebuild of the church on the site of the wooden one that undoubtedly preceded it.

The dedication to St Gregory is also unusual. Gregory was the pope who sent the first Christian mission to Canterbury in 579, which further testifies to the ancient pedigree of this simple but lovely building. The north exterior face of the building is also unusual in that the traditional Tudor brick entrance porch has an identical extension alongside it, which now forms the vestry. The story is that the Lord of the Manor

Ralph Cantrell, a devout Catholic at a time when it became law for all to attend the Protestant church, built this as a private chapel. From here he could sit and listen to the service in the main church through the squint window that is still there today, thus satisfying both the law and his conscience by not actually entering the church.

The beautifully kept interior contains a fine fourteenth-century octagonal font with a partly fifteenth-century wooden cover, a piscina, an enormous rood beam and a very fine set of William and Mary Royal Arms. The stone tomb chest monument to William Cantrell (died 1585), bearing three shields, looks suspiciously like a Catholic altar. Another interesting feature is the ancient iron-bound door in the tower, behind which villagers would have stored their valuables for safety in troubled times. Today, this lovely church is good naturedly left open to all, but my visit was spoiled by one thing. I was shocked to notice that someone had torn the collection box off the wall, smashed the lock and stolen the contents . . . all for a few pennies. How very, very sad!

THE RECONCILIATION HENGRAVE

Originally dedicated to St John Lateran, Hengrave church stands in the grounds of the lovely Hengrave Hall, built by the wealthy merchant Sir Thomas Kytson in the 1530s. It owes its relatively unspoilt condition to an obscure act of law that saved it from excessive Reformation vandalism. The Kytson family were staunchly Catholic and it is a measure of their power and influence that they lavishly entertained Elizabeth I at the Hengrave Hall in 1578. Elizabeth must have had a fondness for this recalcitrant Catholic family. After all, Sir Thomas's father had been a strong supporter of Elizabeth's mother Anne Boleyn, a dangerous stance at the time. Tradition tells that the Queen was taken by the lovely little church and engaged in intense, learned argument with the Kytsons in an attempt to convert them to the Protestant faith. The result was that she failed, and Sir Thomas gave her a jewel instead. In 1589, Elizabeth closed Hengrave as a parish church, purportedly due to its distance from the village boundary, and merged the village with its neighbour Flempton, which became the parish church instead. It is just conceivable that the Queen deliberately and skilfully used the law to enable the Kytsons to bypass the more draconian behaviour of Protestant reformers, making it possible for them to preserve the church as a family mausoleum rather than a place of worship. They continued to maintain a priest, however, and quietly conducted their own private worship here.

The short, wide, tapered round tower indicates a building of Saxon origin, with the chancel probably dating from the thirteenth-century. Further restored by Thomas de Hemegrave in the late fourteenth century, the south side was further altered by the Kytsons in the sixteenth-century. The north side has an aisle with a charming miniature clerestory, the chapel being added in 1540. It is clear how easily the church switched identities to become a mausoleum. The space in the north-east chancel is crammed with family monuments, dominated by the massive six-posted tomb of Margaret Countess of Bath, who died in 1561. She lies dressed in a coronet and red ermine cloak (much of the tomb retains traces of the original colouring), with a greyhound at her feet. By her side, in ruff and armour, lies her third husband John Bouchier Earl of Bath, with his peculiarly modern motto above him, 'Bon temps viendra' ('A good time is coming'). On the shelf beneath them is her first husband, Sir Thomas Kytson, who died in 1552. He lies in knightly armour gazing longingly upwards. Her second husband, Sir Richard Longe is merely represented, almost as an afterthought, by a recessed chest tomb in lieu. One wonders whom he upset. The south-east corner is filled by another massive tomb. This is for Sir Thomas Kytson, who died in 1608. He is lying between his two wives, a stag at the feet of one next to her husband's unicorn. There are also monuments and ornaments to members of the Kytson, Gage and d'Arcy families, including a superb sixteenth-century *Vanitas Moralia* on which a skeleton draws back its shroud, revealing the fragility of the human condition.

In 1900 the church was changed to Anglican worship by Sir John Wood, then passed back to Catholicism in the hands of the Sisters of the Assumption in 1952. In 1974 it was established as an ecumenical retreat and conference centre by a Christian community embracing different Christian denominations and the church was touchingly rededicated to the Reconciliation. This church is unique in the UK, let alone Suffolk, its vivid history, beauty and determined survival making it an essential visit for anyone interested in churches.

Above: The Reconciliation Hengrave

Below left: The tomb of Margaret Countess of Bath

Below middle: The monument to Thomas d'Arcy

Below right: A stag and a unicorn on the tomb of Sir Thomas Kytson

ST MARGARET HERRINGFLEET

St Margaret Herringfleet

This part of North Suffolk could easily be mistaken for Norfolk. A name like Herringfleet conjures up images of a wild sea-lashed fishing port with swooping gulls. In reality we are on the marshes some miles inland and it is unlikely that this was ever a coastal village.

St Margaret is a classic early Norman round tower church built so soon after the Conquest that the builders occasionally lapsed into a more Saxon approach to detail. The tower still boasts its original windows and is topped with bell openings on each side. A thatched nave is met by a similarly thatched porch leading, through the typical Norman doorway complete with zig-zag arch, to a bright clean interior. All is as it should be. Nothing is outstanding or jarring, yet there is plenty of interest. One noteworthy feature is the variety of stained glass to be seen. Although there is some fifteenth-century English work a great deal of it is European, and for some reason comes from the Franciscan priory in Cologne, the pieces being skilfully reset in 1830, probably by Samuel Yarrington of Norwich. Look out for the lovely little fourteenth-century saint in the north wall lancet window, which evidently came from St Olaves Priory.

ALL SAINTS IXWORTH THORPE

Standing on a slight tree-lined rise right next to the busy Ixworth to Thetford road, this pretty little church could easily be mistaken for a farm building. It has a thatched roof that has been extended to cover both the chancel and the nave, which is capped by a weatherboard bell turret. Entering through a redbrick Tudor porch that seems a little large for such a small church, one is confronted with a fairly dark interior (due to the lack of a clerestory) that has been largely but thoughtfully Victorianised. The majority of visitors probably come to see the famous fifteenth-century bench ends. They are special, with rustic depictions of animals and grotesque figures, including a unicorn and mermaid. There is a pleasant Jacobean pulpit and the Norman south doorway represents earlier times.

An unfortunate iron lamppost hogs centre stage outside and seems a strange addition for the parishioners to have allowed to an otherwise picture postcard exterior. Were this church in a more peaceful and secluded spot it would surely be a perfect place for contemplation. In spite of the roar of the traffic this is a place of great interest and simple beauty.

All Saints Ixworth Thorpe

Bernardiston family tombs   The nave   The Bernardiston family pew

The exterior of this church, which is sometimes referred to as 'the Westminster Abbey of Suffolk', gives little indication of the contents of this religious treasure house. Inside the full glory unveils itself: a uniquely intact record of ecclesiastic history spanning over a thousand years.

This is a rather hard, angular building of Norman origin, with a late thirteenth-century nave and chancel and a fourteenth-century tower. From the road it seems uninspiring, yet something about it invites closer inspection. Even for those with an inkling of what to expect, the first glimpse of the interior comes as a revelation. Tombs, pews, pulpit, screens and altar all represent the original glory of their various periods, and are largely untouched by changing religious views or Victorian restoration.

There is no clerestory, but the controversial addition of skylights to the roof in 1857, while not strictly in keeping, does at least provide a lighter interior, highlighting the attractive sixteenth-century hammerbeam roof. Low arcades between the nave and the aisles have piers that were painted in the eighteenth century to give the impression of fluting and above, in each spandrel, there are hatchments, mostly of the Barnardiston family. This Protestant family permeated the history of the church through twenty-seven generations, and there are monuments to them dating from 1503 through to the seventeenth century plus a family vault behind the pulpit which is said to contain fifty more coffins. Although none of the memorials are of outstanding quality and many of the effigies have been defaced, they provide an intriguing record of a dynasty.

During the London apprentice riots in 1641, prior to the Civil War, the Queen's comment on seeing the young Sir Samuel Barnardiston's unusually cropped hair among the rioters 'see what a handsome roundhead is there' gave the Roundheads their name.

Another unique record comes in the form of the hierarchy of the seating, starting with the highly individual, manorial family pew facing the pulpit (rather than the altar). Built about 1610 and incorporating in its structure a lovely fifteenth-century paraclose screen that once stood at the east end of the north aisle, it is divided into two compartments and retains elements of its original colour. It is a highly individual piece. Next in status come the various box pews of the wealthier local families, facing inwards from the aisles, followed then by the simple, well worn bench pews of the villagers, running along both sides of the nave, and finally the children's benches at the end of the nave with peculiar backwards-facing seats for their teachers.

The octagonal three-decker pulpit, dating from 1610, still retains its wig-stand and an hourglass for timing sermons. Standing high on a turned pedestal measuring barely twenty-six inches across, it was never designed for a corpulent vicar. From here the hopefully thin puritan Samuel Fairclough delivered his fiery and very lengthy rhetoric to packed houses. Beyond is the 1620s screen, the oldest post-Reformation screen in the country, and behind the altar, above a fine 1930s retable, is a lovely Saxon crucifix. Discovered under the floor in the early nineteenth-century, it makes a further statement in this wonderful monument to past times.

ST PETER AND ST PAUL KEDINGTON

St Peter and St Paul Kedington

ST MARY AND ST PETER KELSALE

St Mary and St Peter Kelsale

The lychgate

To wander on a sunlit day along a twisting lane that leads through the lovely lychgate into a glorious churchyard with avenues of pollarded lime trees is an experience not to be missed.

Here is a church that, while Norman in origin, also represents some of the finest work of the Arts and Crafts Movement to be found in the county, if not the country. A fifteenth-century porch welcomes without hinting at the surprises that it will reveal. Open the door, with its massive iron knocker, and enter an interior flooded with light from a west window that compensates for the lack of a clerestory. Here is a treasure trove of ancient and modern, side by side in seamless harmony. When the nave was widened in the fourteenth-century the Norman entrance door, with its eye-catching carved arch, was simply reused in the north wall of the nave. Under a scissor-beamed roof the unusually large fifteenth-century font is backed by a massive and interesting 1881 septych, originally a reredos, but moved to its present position because it blocked the light from the east window. This interesting piece depicts, in seven panels, events from the lives of St Mary and St Peter along with the Tree of Life, the Tree of Knowledge and the Tree of Shame.

The nave and chancel

This church was the subject of two restorations in the 1870s, the first by Richard Norman Shaw (who designed New Scotland Yard) and the second by his pupil E.S. Prior shortly after. Prior not only added false gargoyles, the wonderful lychgate and a fine rood group, but dictated the overall flavour of this virtuoso ensemble building. Under him the nave and chancel gained some windows by famous names such as William Morris, Ford Madox Browne and Edward Burne-Jones. A fine wrought-iron screen, which complements the seventeenth-century pulpit, looks down not on traditional pews, but on Prior's distinctive oak benches 'designed along the lines of superior garden furniture', according to Mortlock. The changes that time has wrought on this church are unique in the way they have been integrated. A coat of arms of Queen Victoria proclaims approval of the comfortable marriage of styles this lovely building offers.

The font and septych

The nave and chancel

The tomb of Sir William Cordell

Stained glass

At the time of the Domesday Book this was already a thriving place. Sheep were the currency that created the wealth, and that wealth paid for the splendour of this church. By medieval times, Long Melford and nearby Lavenham were among the richest towns in Europe and the competition for grandeur between the two churches can still be perceived today. Holy Trinity proclaimed itself through the benefice of three wealthy families who became its patrons: the Cloptons, the Cordells and the Martyns. Such is the glory of this church that even Pevsner waxes lyrical about it, pronouncing it one of the most moving parish churches in England: 'large, proud and noble'.

To get a feel of the building, approach it through the churchyard and walk completely round, resisting for a while the urge to go inside. Simply feel the scale and remember that this is not a cathedral, but a parish church. All that is left of the earlier building are parts of the nave arcades; most of the present structure was built in a well documented sequence. Work started around 1460 and nothing externally is older than that. In 1481 the tall transomed clerestory was built. In 1484 the south chapel was added. In 1496 the Cloptons, possibly using the same architect who designed St Nicholas Denston, extended the arcades to nine bays and added the beautiful Lady Chapel, with its three parallel pitched roofs. The tower comes as a complete surprise. It is modern, built in 1898–1903, a brilliantly skilful encasement in flint and stone of the eighteenth-century redbrick tower that had surely replaced something earlier still.

The entrance, via the south porch, leads into a massive interior filled with light. The only purpose of the walls seems to be to support the wealth of glass. To get an idea of the effect this interior must have had in medieval times, remember that everything would then have been richly coloured. The unquestioned glory of this church is the fifteenth-century stained glass – a pageant of people, fashions and beliefs of medieval England. In the nineteenth century the stained glass was collected together in the east window and aisles, but it was completely rearranged in the 1960s and displayed to perfection in the north aisle, a unique collection of martyrs, saints and portraits of local dignitaries, such as Elizabeth Talbot, on whom Tenniel is said to have based the Duchess when illustrating Lewis Caroll's *Alice in Wonderland*. It is a measure of the power of the Clopton, Cordell and Martyn families that so much that is wonderful in this church survived the iconoclastic excesses that followed. Each family has its own chapel in which they are well represented by elaborate tombs, brasses and memorials.

The Lady Chapel is in a class of its own; indeed, one has to exit the main church and enter the chapel by a small side door on the south side. A gem of architectural virtuosity, it was used as a school from 1670 until the early nineteenth century, evidence of which is to be seen in the large multiplication table painted on the wall. Today, as Simon Jenkins points out, it must be Britain's grandest Sunday school.

There is so much to see in this wonderful church that further description would read like an inventory. One final noteworthy point is that Holy Trinity, for all its treasures, is not a museum but an active living church, as it always has been.

HOLY TRINITY LONG MELFORD

Holy Trinity Long Melford

The font

The rood screen

St John the Baptist Lound

The organ case

Wall painting of St Christopher

ST JOHN THE BAPTIST LOUND

The nave and chancel

Widely known as the 'Golden Church', this is a church that might enrage the purist but will enthral all others. Pevsner, in peevish understatement, grants that 'the interior is made festive by much recent furnishing and sham Gothic pieces,' which is to miss the point entirely. Like it or loathe it, there is nothing sham here.

The building started out as a Norman round tower church with the usual fourteenth-century additions plus an unsatisfactory thatched roof. What little was left by Reformation vandalism constituted nothing special in 1827, when it was visited by the historian David Elisha Davy and all was falling into disrepair. A partial restoration took place in 1873, and another in 1875. A hint of what the future was to hold came with the addition of a fine north window in 1893 followed by another on the south side in 1904, the work of Henry Holiday, the celebrated Pre-Raphaelite painter known for his skill in stained glass.

In 1908 a new rector, Father Booth Lynes, arrived and, thanks to his devotion to his little church, coupled with the genius of his choice of restorer, Sir Ninian Comper, all was to change forever. In 1912, funding the project almost entirely himself, Booth Lynes commissioned Comper to transform the church to a style approaching their perception of its original medieval splendour. Using the considerable skills of H.A. Barnard to paint and gild under his supervision, Comper set about the huge task with enthusiasm. The high altar was raised on new flooring and gorgeously decorated posts were added, topped with gilded angels carrying torches. These supported curtains of Spanish silk, dyed Comper's trademark pink. The curtains were decorated with a profusion of religious imagery, such as Jesus blessing his people, flanked by the two Johns — a sumptuous backdrop for those receiving the bread and wine of the daily mass.

Next came the font, to which a cover was added, a fabulous gilded steeple suspended from a decorated beam with a hoist for raising and lowering it. Then, a large St Christopher was painted in its traditional position on the north wall opposite the entrance. But this was no ordinary St Christopher. To the usual symbols of travel Comper added himself driving his Rolls Royce, and, when the mural was restored in 1964 a representation of a Bristol Britannia aircraft was revealed. After this came the remarkable rood screen with Jesus crucified on a tree attended by the Virgin and a disciple surrounded by cherubim and with dragons (symbolising evil) at the foot of the cross. Comper's love of medieval heraldry and his modern vision of it is displayed everywhere. In 1913 came the final touch: the splendid organ case at the west ends of the church, executed with Gothic and Baroque styles combined in what Comper described as 'the unity of inclusion' (whatever that might mean).

All was finished just as the First World War started, an end, forever, of things as they had been for centuries. It may be that Comper's vision looked too longingly at past times. Yet perhaps his finest work was still to come. In 1920 he was asked to design the crucifix on the exterior, south wall of the nave: the village memorial to the fallen. To a countryside devastated by human loss he gave back some beauty through the courage and glory of his imagination.

ST MARY MELLIS

Carved heads on the interior and exterior

What a strange spot this is. Despite the Diss to London trains rushing by, the village, divided by a sweeping green, seems to be in the middle of nowhere. The church itself is not easy to find and you might easily pass it a number of times before finally spotting it hidden behind trees well outside the village.

The tower collapsed in 1730, leaving the truncated building looking more like a sturdy medieval fortress than a church. The feeling now is that it must have been a much more important building in its heyday. The two-storey porch in the Decorated style leads into an unusually wide nave with large, Perpendicular, three-light windows. Some of the glass in the south windows has fifteenth-century figures and heads in the tracery. The Perpendicular font is carved with four lions and four Tudor roses. The table tombs, one to a Richard Yaxley, 1570, have all had their coats of arms obliterated and their brasses stripped. Inside and outside the building are carved heads with peculiar expressions from various periods. Although the interior is big it is somehow not that imposing.

The real attraction of this unusual church is the visual impression given by its unusual external statement, which might be compared to a huge Crusading knight.

St Mary Mellis

ST MARY MILDENHALL

St Mary Mildenhall

The timber roof

A carved angel on one of the tie beams

The tomb of Sir Henry North

Lakenheath airbase often provides a mind-dulling background of noise to what would otherwise be a typical Suffolk market town. St Mary is a huge church, Suffolk's biggest, and actually the largest medieval building in the county. Situated right in the centre of the old town, its awesome grandeur is somewhat eclipsed by being hemmed in on all sides. Although there was an earlier church here, the oldest part of the present building is probably the Early English style vestry, but the main shell was built in 1220. Enlargements were made and new windows added about 1300 and the nave, aisles and porches were constructed about 1420. The magnificent west tower, rising 120 feet above the town, was completed in 1460 and on a fine day the spire of Ely Cathedral can be seen from the top. The churchyard has a rare charnel house chapel, a necessity in medieval towns where space was at a premium. To make way for new burials, corpses were dug up after a suitable period and the remains placed in charnel houses, where a special priest guarded them and said masses for them. The practice died out after the Reformation.

Entry is usually through the inspiring two-storey north porch, the largest in the UK. The upper floor has reverted to its original use as a chapel but at one time it served as a school. The large lower ceiling has wonderful vaulting with many carved bosses. In 1519, a Thomas Marchanter left 20d for 'reparacions of the chapel of Owre Lady ovyr the porche'.

Once inside it takes a moment to adjust to the sheer size. There is the mighty tower, above which are four chambers, and a stone minstrel gallery, which is open to the nave and forms a perfect frame for the lovely east window. The nave roof is low pitched. Tie beams alternate with hammerbeams carved with large angels with outspread wings. The craftsmanship is fabulous but that of the lean-to roofs of the aisles is even more impressive. It is awesome. A mass of angels, biblical scenes, symbols and all manner of human and animal representations decorate the roof supports. This is a marriage of great ecclisiastic art and total functionality. Much of the carving has suffered iconoclastic mutilation and records for 1651 show that a man was paid a shilling a day to destroy all 'superstitious' symbols. Those too high up were shot at by Parliamentary soldiers, brought in to finish the job.

In the south aisle there is a splendid alabaster tomb of Sir Henry North, died 1620. He lies in effigy alongside his wife, their six children kneeling in front. Another interesting altar tomb is that of Sir Henry Barton, Lord Mayor of London in 1416 and again in 1428. He would almost certainly have known Dick Whittington, who was Lord Mayor in 1419. This tomb is a cenotaph tomb since Sir Henry is actually buried in St Paul's Cathedral.

There is so much to see and so much of value in this church that, for once, it is not surprising that it is kept locked. But a key can be obtained from the shoe shop barely fifty yards away.

ST PETER MONK SOHAM

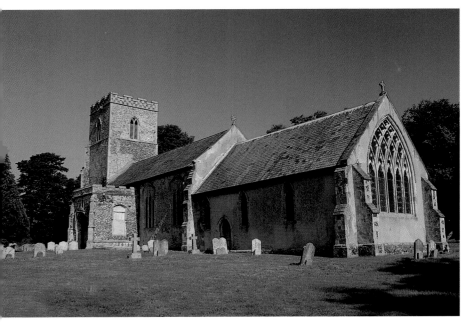

St Peter Monk Soham

View across rape fields

Monk Soham was founded as a contemplative retreat for the monks of nearby Bury St Edmunds, probably after the Norman Conquest. And what a retreat! My first sight of it, across a half-mile track weaving through bright yellow rape fields crowned by a clear blue sky, was breathtaking, as it will be at any season of the year. From the road, the first glimpses are of the top of the thirteenth-century tower. One approach is from a small signpost pointing across an open field. There can be few churches with such a wonderfully invigorating approach.

Once the peaceful churchyard is reached, anticipation has already fixed the mind to appreciate whatever is there, and there is plenty to satisfy expectations. The strong, silent, contemplative building spans a number of distinct architectural periods. The porch, although less than well preserved, has pleasant chequerboard flushwork with a mixture of heraldry and empty niches. The Y-tracery of the tower dates it to around 1300 and the interior, full of light, further echoes a long history. The hammerbeam roof of the nave has arch braces that do not start from the end of hammerbeams, making them 'structurally wasted'. This seems to be a peculiarity. The rood beam is still in place and an interesting pulpit is from the very early the Jacobean period, being dated 1604. A massive 10-foot-long iron chest lies on the floor behind the font. But it is the font itself that is the pride of this interior. Although the panels are largely mutilated, this is a glorious seven-sacrament font said to be fourteenth-century but quite probably older.

This is a church that should be visited as much for the delightful experience of the walk to its open and welcoming front door as for anything else.

ST PETER MOULTON

St Peter Moulton

St Peter is worth seeing not so much for its beauty or architectural integrity, but more for its hauntingly idyllic location. It stands high above the south end of this lovely village surrounded by rolling fields full of grazing sheep and majestically overlooking the River Kennet, with its famous medieval packhorse bridge, now alas spanning a dry riverbed.

This was once a wide, tall Norman building, and twelfth-century columns are still to be seen where the nave meets the chancel at the west end of the church. A late thirteenth-century tower commands the view but the body of the building is sixteenth-century with a very unsympathetic restoration having been carried out in 1850. One interesting peculiarity is found in the vestry: an ancient stone carving of two figures, a man with arms raised, possibly in prayer, and a woman with her hands folded over her belly.

A walk along the towpath of the riverbed, glancing up at the church standing triumphantly on its mound, witness to countless ages of admiring glances, justifies a visit.

ST ANDREW MUTFORD

St Andrew Mutford

This church was almost made redundant in 1973 but the local parishioners fought to keep it open and happily won the day. An important piece of history was saved.

On a very steep bank alongside the road, looking even taller than it actually is, the church is approached by a short climb to a gate which opens on to an unusual first aspect. An imposing Galilee porch, the only one to be found on a round tower church, stands head on, slightly off centre of the actual tower and giving a slightly lopsided effect to the building. A Galilee porch is so called because it was the final 'station' in processions around the building. Heading the procession, the priest symbolised Christ leading his disciples into Galilee after the Resurrection. Similar Calvary processions can still be seen at the time of religious festivals in many parts of Brittany today.

The Domesday Book mentions two churches at Mutford but there is no indication of the other. St Andrew is of Saxon origin; certainly the tower is Saxon. At 66 feet it is the tallest and possibly most beautiful of all round towers. The octagonal belfry was added in the fourteenth century but if anything adds to the majesty of the original while the lovely setting compliments the strong statement made by the building. Mostly built in the fourteenth century, this church was nearly derelict until a 1930s restoration slowly began to give it new life.

Stepping inside on to the lovely pale brick floor there is plenty to see, especially the font with its inscription telling that it was donated by Dame Elizabeth of Hengrave in 1380. There are some fine poppyhead benches and traces of wall painting, which not so very long ago could be clearly seen, but which are now barely distinguishable.

The noble exterior of this church is so compelling that it is worth a visit just to experience the extraordinary head-on vision on entering the gate.

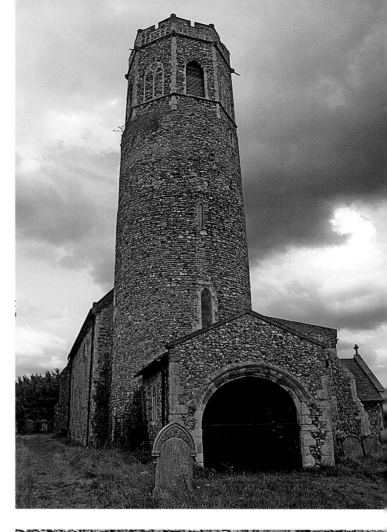

Above: The Galilee porch

Right: Tombstones in the churchyard

ST JOHN THE BAPTIST ONEHOUSE

Onehouse has a detailed Domesday Book entry, but it is a surprise the Normans ever found the place. The quaintly lovely church is isolated and little visited. It is half a mile up a dirt track from a village whose two parts are miles from each other.

It is well worth locating, and the view of it lying in the distance across shining fields is especially enticing. The building is neither spectacular nor imposing, but simple, serene and peaceful. The tower, Norman according to Pevsner but more likely Saxon, joins a fifteenth-century nave with a more ancient south porch. The understated interior boasts an ancient font. Nothing shouts out here except the silence and the church blends in with its surroundings as if it had stood here for ever.

St John the Baptist Onehouse

The nave

The memorial tablet to Jacob Brand

The Royal Arms

It may only be legend that the ancient 'gospel oak' in the churchyard was planted by St Cede, but since there is no evidence of an early church it could be that the oak was a place for early preaching. The church was built in the early part of the reign of Henry II, in *c.*1160. There are those who believe that the Norman builders reused Roman bricks in the construction but although Roman coins have been found in the area this is not at all certain.

Above the entrance arch is the characteristic Norman zig-zag decoration, but many of St Mary's other Norman vestiges have nothing else like them in the county, for example the very rare brick arches, built on pillars of dressed stone with carved capitals, and the brick clerestory. Alterations were first made at the end of the fourteenth century, when the clerestory windows were blocked, the roof of the chancel was raised and Decorative style windows were added, along with the two porches. This work was carried out by the Lambourne family, Lords of the Manor at the time, and it is thought that the carved heads either side of the north doorway are those of the benefactor and his wife. Further restoration took place in 1510–20, adding to an already fascinating interior. On the wall above the lovely pulpit, between arches that from every angle give a different perspective to this lovely interior, there is a memorial tablet dated 1630 with coloured figures – a kneeling man with a small boy. This is Jacob Brand, Lord of the Manor, and his son Benjamin, who is believed to have died after falling out of a window at Polstead Hall. There is also a unique brick font standing on thirteenth-century

supports, some interesting brasses, an ancient door with a sanctuary ring and even the remains of a wall painting. How did all this survive Dowsing's visit in April 1643?

Outside, the individuality continues. The tower has Suffolk's only surviving stone spire. Rising 73 feet into the sky, it miraculously survived the devastating storm of 1987. On the south porch there is a scratch dial, which, for some unknown reason, is upside down. The magic of this church is the sum of its parts rather than any individual feature. Everything about it is unique.

The parish register lists the names of several villagers who sailed with the pilgrims for America in the Mayflower and further tells that, while the plague of 1626 claimed ten people from the village, the Great Plague of 1665 claimed none. This is also the village of the notorious Red Barn Murder that shook England in 1827, when Maria Marten, the daughter of the local molecatcher, was brutally murdered. Maria was buried here but all trace of her tombstone has long gone to souvenir hunters. Meanwhile, William Corder, the murderer, was hanged and flayed and a full report of the trial was printed on his skin, which is still to be seen in Bury Museum. Another person now resting in the lovely churchyard is Percy Edwards, the renowned animal impersonator, who provided all the animals sounds in radio shows such as *Ray's a Laugh*, and went on to work in television and film. He provided the voice of the monster in the film *Alien*. He could impersonate the calls of six hundred different birds, so what more fitting place for him than this lovely hillside, with its chorus of his beloved birdsong?

ST MARY POLSTEAD

St Mary Polstead

ALL SAINTS RAMSHOLT

All Saints Ramsholt

The nave and chancel

This is an ancient and mysterious place but in medieval times, when Edward III's fleet was moored in the estuary below, this would have been a thriving and busy settlement.

This picturesquely evocative church stands totally alone about a mile from the road, nestled high above the marshes of the Deben estuary and silhouetted against an often angry sky – a location that would be hard to match for pure romantic atmosphere. Here is another church well worth seeking out. Apparently this spot is no longer as lonely as it was a few years ago but if seen, as it was when I visited, with not another soul in sight, it is impossible not to feel the drama it presents.

There was probably a church on this spot long before the Norman Conquest and, on first glance, the present building is an imposing but straightforward early Norman (or possibly late Saxon) round tower church, constructed from undressed flint, brick and the local brown septaria stone found on the beaches and cliffs in the area. However, closer inspection reveals that this tower is in fact oval, and the unusual buttressing, reaching all the way to the top, makes it one of only two such towers in Suffolk, the other being at Boyton.

The interior is bright and pleasant, if a little bland, with a fourteenth-century piscina and a pretty drop sill sedilia in the sanctuary. Entry to the tower is through a Norman doorway, beside which stands a font with a fifteenth-century bowl on a Norman base. Lying alongside it is what appears to be a fine thirteenth-century stone coffin, but it was actually used for washing and preparing the dead before burial.

Anyone with an interest in ecclesiastical buildings, history or inspiringly romantic settings should beat a path to the door of this church.

The font

The nave and chancel

This sturdy building surrounded by the remains of a moat was never intended to be a simple parish church but was originally part of a Benedictine Priory founded in 1064. Although a modest monastery, it must have stood in quite an impressive location at the time of the Norman Conquest. Today the church is hedged in by all the trappings of modern village expansion.

The founding cell survived until just after the Conquest, when Stigand the Archbishop of Canterbury was deposed and his estates transferred to William de Noyers. Rumburgh passed to Alan the Red, Earl of Richmond, then to his brother Alan the Black, who presented it to St Mary's Abbey in York. It remained under the abbey's auspices until 1528, when Henry VIII granted it to Cardinal Wolsey who used the revenues to fund his college at Ipswich. Wolsey's term of ascendancy was short and his college was dissolved in 1530. In 1538 the whole area was purchased by the Duke of Norfolk. It was again confiscated by Henry VIII when Norfolk fell out of favour, but it was restored to him in 1553. Throughout the changing ownership this church has stood strong and resolute. Once

the priory had gone it took its place as a humble parish church, with an air of confident austerity.

The very unusual truncated thirteenth-century tower with its low, angled buttresses is much wider than it is deep and stands head on to the approaching visitor — impressive in its simplicity. Above a peculiarly small central door are three tall, widely spaced windows, the central one taller than the other two, all of this capped by a weatherboard belfry under a high pitched roof. It is a matter of debate whether the tower was unfinished, and this belfry was a replacement for an earlier damaged top to the tower, or whether it was simply designed as it is. Whatever the answer, the tower works. Unusually, the tall chancel and nave are the same width as the tower. Entry is through a fifteenth-century porch with a simple, almost insignificant twelfth-century inner doorway. The interior is unexpectedly cold. Its glory must have been the beautiful high ogee arched screen; the medieval colour now, alas, varnished over, it shows only faint traces of the former beauty of the original gesso work. On the right of the tower are the arms of George III while on the left are the original arms of the priory, discovered during rebuilding work in 1878. Among many other things to be noted are a Jacobean pulpit that, until 1896, stood in the centre of the nave, and a fourteenth-century font. This is a unique building, which has weathered a chequered history.

Before leaving look, for the simple, stoic epitaph to Elizabeth Davy who died in 1781, aged only twenty-one.

> She once the fairest flower of May,
> Now turned to lifeless clay;
> Good god what can we say,
> He calls we must obey.

ST MICHAEL AND ST FELIX RUMBURGH

St Michael and St Felix Rumburgh

ST NICHOLAS RUSHBROOKE

St Nicholas Rushbrooke

The box stalls and Royal Arms

The font

The monument to Thomas Jermyn

Momento mori

At a single glance, this church, tucked away across ploughed fields, demands closer scrutiny. Lying in a hamlet caringly rebuilt by Lord Rothschild in 1955–63, it is largely the inspired fantasy of a Colonel Rushbrooke in the mid-nineteenth century. The tower is fourteenth-century and much of the rest is fifteenth-century, with a chancel rebuilt by Thomas Jermyn in the 1540s. However, it is the fantastic, eccentric interior that holds all the surprises. This is arguably the most unusual church interior in Suffolk, if not the country.

On entering there is a distinct feel of the theatre about the place – the perfect setting for a Civil War drama. Collegiate-style seating of dark wooden box stalls, incorporating medieval poppyhead bench ends, integrate with some fine medieval stained glass, missing brasses and other older remnants, with amazing ease. A fine inscribed rood beam (archaically spelt 'Dieu en Mon Droict'), ornate heraldry and monuments throughout, further the impression of a time warp, adding to the general air of mystery. Much of the wood panelling is thought to have come from the original moated Tudor hall, which was mysteriously destroyed by fire, then demolished without permission in 1961. Its loss was lamented as a 'great calamity' by Pevsner. This church is undoubtedly a confection, but a very moving and inspired one. The purely decorative organ pipes have no instrument attached,

but nevertheless play their part in the overall design of an interior that ought not to work, but somehow does. Nothing here is exactly what it seems.

On the east wall is a fine carved stone effigy of the last of the Jermyn family. This is Thomas Jermyn, who died aged fifteen when a mast fell on his head while boating on the River Thames in 1692. A further mystery, and a matter of heated contention, concerns the huge and completely unique carved and painted Royal Arms of Henry VIII in the tympanum above the rood beam. To find any Tudor coat of arms in a church is very rare, and this is the only surviving one from Henry VIII's reign in the whole of England (Mary I having had all of them destroyed along with those of her brother Edward VI). Was this amazing piece originally made for this church, put in when Thomas Jermyn was granted the estate by Henry VIII in 1540? The problem here is that records show that it certainly was not in the church in the early nineteenth century. There are various theories, but it does not push credibility too far to believe that the arms *were* originally in the church, and that they were simply removed and hidden, perhaps at the hall, during the reign of Mary I. Stored and forgotten, they were rediscovered by Colonel Rushbrooke and reinstalled in their present position.

The monument to Dame Margrett Tylney

The carved bench ends

Barely in Suffolk, All Saints Shelley, with its nearby hall, should not be confused with the church and hall of the same name not far away in Essex. It is tucked away in an area where you would not expect to find such a beautiful village, close to the thundering highways that serve East Anglia.

Unusually, the fourteenth-century north tower appears to be behind the church. One enters the building from the south, up a short path and through a charming, quaintly rustic, Tudor porch. The interior is a continuation of the simple and direct charm of the entire building. A wonderful Elizabethan linenfold pulpit looms over the congregation, looking directly down on the simple, yet serene effigy of Dame Margrett Tylney, built to her memory by her son Phillip and dated 1598.

Nearby Shelley Hall is what remains of the mansion of Sir Philip Tylney, a distant relative of Anne Boleyn and a notable local personage. Sir Phillip died in 1533 but, while there is an ornate square panel monument bearing various Tylney heraldry in the north chancel, it bears no inscription. Despite the crests and arms of the Tylney family being evident everywhere, memorials to the other Tylneys remain elusive, with no mention of Sir Phillip, and certainly nothing approaching the physical presence of Dame Margrett's fine effigy. Is there a story behind this?

On the north wall to the east are the remains of a Tudor brick chapel dating from about 1530, with substantial sections of elaborate wood panelling. Beautifully carved bench ends again carry the Tylney arms alongside other fine carvings. This church clearly had a very different

layout before the Reformation and the remote location probably accounts for its retaining many aspects of past eras, unlike so many Suffolk churches that were defaced by future religious bigots. Although Dowsing did pay a fairly destructive visit here, the damage was limited.

An endearing surprise awaits outside: the totally out-of-key peel of what at first sounds like distant church bells, but is actually the chiming clock, which replaced the original bells in 1904. This strange tunelessness somehow adds to the overall sense of rustic beauty of the place. There is history and timeless community here and it is clear that this lovely building has served its village well throughout its life, and continues to do so.

In 2005 archaeologists working at the early fort in Jamestown USA unearthed a male skeleton they believe to be Captain Bartholomew Gosnold of Suffolk. In 1602 Gosnold obtained a charter from James I to settle Virginia and, leading a small expedition, he established the first, short-lived, English settlement in America. The Church of England recently gave permission for achaeologists to dig up the remains of Gosnold's sister, Elizabeth Gosnold Tilney, who was buried at Shelley, and extract DNA samples for comparison with the skeleton at Jamestown. If the DNA matches it is almost certain they have the remains of Gosnold and he will take his rightfully important place in history as the earliest and most influential spirit in the English colonization of America, a much earlier founding father of modern America than the Pilgrim Fathers who went over in the *Mayflower* later.

ALL SAINTS SHELLEY

All Saints Shelley

ST JOHN THE BAPTIST SNAPE

St John the Baptist Snape

Once closer to the sea than it is today, Snape is in an area of estuaries and salt marshes, buzzing with wildlife. In 1862, a 48-foot Saxon longboat, contemporary with that at Sutton Hoo, was discovered here, giving testament to an ancient maritime heritage. Snape is the location of the famous Aldeburgh Festival founded by Benjamin Britten in the 1960s, which is held at the Maltings. Unfortunately the church stands a brisk walk from the Maltings and only a conscious decision to visit brings most visitors to its door. This is a pity because, after a visit to the more popular Maltings, this lovely little church rounds things off with a tranquil view of the sort of thing that attracted Britten to the area.

There has been a church here since 1085, but the oldest fabric to be seen today is early thirteenth-century. The tower was begun in the 1440s, with battlements being added in *c*.1525. The chancel has seen many changes but was recorded as being 'in a very ruinous condition' in 1602. The Victorians did very little restoration so by 1920 the condition was such that the building had to be heavily buttressed to prevent collapse. Since then it has been lovingly restored. Entering through the pretty fourteenth-century porch with a Lamb of God depicted above, a generous welcome is extended by an uncluttered and lovingly cared-for interior. This simple building boasts no imposing aisles or clerestory but what it lacks in grandeur it makes up for with innocent hospitality.

Dowsing was here in 1643 and, although he smashed windows and removed four brasses, he thankfully missed some important items. The font probably escaped his attention by having the imagery craftily plastered over before his arrival. Thanks to that, a very interesting late fifteenth-century font was saved reasonably intact when the plaster was removed. It is decorated with lions, lizards and a dedication to the donors, the Mey family, who are shown in one of the panels alongside the Trinity, the idolatry of which would have really upset Dowsing. Interestingly, money was given in 1520 for colouring the font. What must it have looked like in all its illuminated glory? Dowsing also appears to have missed a very important fifteenth-century brass of five little girls. Unfortunately this was stolen from the church in recent times, but a rubbing of it is now in the British Museum. A very pretty new organ and a charming gallery complete the picture.

The nave and chancel

The font

ST EDMUND SOUTHWOLD

The nave and chancel

Until the sea finally closed the harbour, Southwold was a prosperous fishing port. It is now a retirement and holiday destination. The uniqueness of this very grand church is that, unlike most, it is the result of one continuous building operation throughout the fifteenth century, a time when the town could conspicuously display its growing wealth in the beauty of its parish church. And what beauty they achieved.

Building started in 1430 after the small thirteenth-century chapel that had served the community was burnt to the ground. There are legacies that record the building progress and it is possible to follow the construction with some continuity. The magnificent tower, a masterly display of flintwork rising 100 feet into the sky, counterbalances the 144-foot nave to perfection. A superb vaulted two-storey south porch, an amazing eighteen-light clerestory and a pretty sanctus bell turret (reconstructed in 1867), set upon a green

copper roof, form a breathtaking whole. New prosperity fired the whole project and it shows in every aspect of this masterpiece.

By 1460 it was time to concentrate on the interior and on entering through the lovely early Tudor linenfold door, it is impossible not to stare in wonder at what was achieved. Everywhere there is colour and history. The hammerbeam roof rests on a host of carved angels that change from plain wood to glorious colour as they finally reach the chancel to rest beneath a canopy of honour ceiling, painted blue and dotted with golden stars. Below all this, the famous screen unusually spans both aisles and the chancel arch. The north aisle screen has a rare set of medieval panels painted with orders of angels. The chancel arch screen has further panels, thought to be the work of the Norwich School, depicting the apostles, while the south aisle is the work of yet another hand and, unusually for Suffolk, depicts Old Testament prophets. Such is the difference in the workmanship that it has been suggested that they came from other churches. Nevertheless they are not misfits here.

The font cover, covering a seven sacrament font, was designed by Comper's pupil F.E. Howard, sumptuously painted and gilded and, at 24 feet high, the tallest in England. It dwarfs even that at Ufford, yet blends into this place gracefully. There is also a fabulously carved fifteenth-century wineglass pulpit and a lovely west window designed in 1954 by Comper, one of his last works. Magical fifteenth-century misericords and choir stalls display English woodcarving at it's finest — poppyheads, animals, even a man who appears to be suffering from toothache, complemented by lavishly carved armrests and canopies. As you leave, a final treat remains. On the wall next to the tower arch is 'Southwold Jack', the fifteenth-century mechanical clock, a fine example of an original carved and coloured wooden figure. Dressed in the armour of his day, he records each hour by striking a bell with his battleaxe.

The pulpit

The painted screen

The font cover

The hammerbeam roof

The chancel

The font

The doom painting

ST NICHOLAS STANNINGFIELD

This is a sturdy church with a massively imposing, if somewhat squat, fourteenth-century tower. Was it unfinished or was it designed this way? Pevsner thought the thirteenth-century chancel 'uncommonly interesting', adding, in a rare outburst of facetiousness, that 'the designer certainly liked personal tracery'. The earliest part of the building is the Norman nave, which has an unusually asymmetrical fifteenth-century screen displaying some fine carving on both sides. There are some nicely carved poppyhead benches too. Above the screen are the sad remains of a doom painting in a poor state of repair and needing urgent attention if it is not to deteriorate past the point of restoration. A fourteenth-century font is decorated with the Rokewood arms and it was a fourteenth-century bequest from this family that built the chancel, in which there is a fine canopied table tomb, thought to be that of Thomas Rokewood (died 1521) who was married to Anne, the daughter of John Clopton of Kentwell (Long Melford). The tomb displays the Rokewood arms alongside those of the Clerbecke, Swynbourne and Clopton families and the monument serves as a reminder of the carefully maintained dynastic interplay between wealthy medieval families.

The Rokewoods of Coldham Hall dominate this church and the surrounding area and are part of the same family that owned and lost Euston. They were also related by marriage to that other unshakably Catholic family, the Gages of Hengrave. In 1605 one of the Rokewood family lost his life for involvement in the Gunpowder Plot, and their star shone less brightly from then on. Somehow the Rokewoods kept their faith alive, surviving the many persecutions and troubled times they lived through, yet managing to at least keep hold of Coldham Hall until the last of the line fell in the First World War. The hall now belongs to a supermodel, an intriguing tick of the clock of history.

ST MARY STOKE BY NAYLAND

St Mary Stoke by Nayland

The tomb of Sir Francis Mannock

The south doors

The font

A superb church that holds an acclaimed place midway between the grand and the small churches of Suffolk. Simon Jenkins, in his *Thousand Best Churches*, rightly rhapsodises about the ornate tower, but there is so much more here. The date of the tower is disputed but 1460s is probably reasonably accurate. Between 1439 and 1459 money was left by wealthy local families for the building of a tower and what was eventually erected is a masterpiece of architectural dignity achieved by medieval builders. The redbrick fabric is crowned by crocketed stone pinnacles climbing above mammoth stepped buttresses flanking the corners. Canopied niches once held religious figures. Sadly they have disappeared due to the zealous attention of various reformers. Windows grace all sides of the tower, beautifully balanced and pouring light into the interior.

The first impression given by the interior is the scale. Looking back along the nave towards the tower, a fabulously tall, slim, tower arch frames the stained glass window of the opposite wall commanding the space. The clerestory and the wealth of other windows throughout ensure that the nave, aisles and chancel hold few dark corners.

In the south chapel, among other memorials, is the tomb of Lady Anne Windsor (died 1615). Carved in alabaster, she lies richly robed, her two daughters at her head, her son at her feet. Illustrating the ugliness of fundamentalist bigotry, Parliamentary officers broke off the hands of the female figures in 1643, because they were in

represented in a 'superstitious' attitude of prayer. The north chapel holds the tomb of Sir Francis Mannock (died 1634), which is thought to be the work of Nicholas Stone. The Mannocks were a committed Catholic family who, for recusancy (not attending the established church), forfeited two thirds of their estate in 1596. During restoration work in 1965 a vault was discovered to the front of this memorial. It contained the lead coffins of Sir William and Sir Thomas Mannock (the 5th and 8th Baronets), their wives and an infant. The remains were reinterred in the same vault. Spread about the church are a number of important brasses, the earliest and finest being Sir William de Tendring. It states that he died in 1408, which cannot be, since it is known he fought at Agincourt in 1415.

There are two porches, the north Tudor porch and the two-storey south porch, through which most people enter. Though restored, this porch is probably earlier than most of the building. It houses the remains of the old parish library on its upper floor and boasts the most beautifully carved oak doors to be seen anywhere in the country. These lovingly crafted fifteenth-century treasures are thought to depict the lineage of Christ in a Tree of Jesse that swarms with marvellous figures, foliage, birds, insects and intricate tracery. Put simply, they are a masterpiece.

There is so much to see in this wonderful church that you should allow plenty of time for your visit.

The nave and chancel

The monument to
Sir Michael Stanhope

The organ

All Saints is just two miles from the sea, as near to Orford as to Sudbourne, with the forest to the north, the rectory to the east and, to the south and west, flat, open fields as far as the eye can see. The salt of the sea is always in the air and a distant glimpse of the sun sparkling off the gilded weathercock acts as a magnet, making it impossible to pass this lovely church, located in such a beautiful setting, without going for a closer look.

There was once a Saxon church here, probably wooden, but mention of two churches in the Domesday Book is curious, for there is no trace of the other. The core of the present building, especially the south wall, is early twelfth-century. In the first part of the fourteenth century a tower was added with Perpendicular style windows being added to the nave and both porches in the fifteenth century. There is a record that in 1621 the church was thatched but by 1870 the whole building was very dilapidated.

The manor had been purchased from the Crown by the Stanhope family. It passed in the seventeenth century to the Devereux, Viscounts of Hereford, then in the 1750s to the Seymours, who were Marquises of Hertford, and then to Sir Richard Wallace, who bought the manor in 1871 from his 'natural' father, Gerard Seymour Marquis of Hertford. (Sir Richard Wallace inherited the collection of treasures in Hertford's London home which became the now famous Wallace Collection.) Total restoration took place in 1878–9, instigated by Sir Richard. During these restorations, Wallace donated some fine glass and the splendid organ, and had the tower topped with a lead-covered spirelet, which is a common feature in Hertfordshire, known as a 'Hertfordshire spike'.

He probably added this touch in honour of his father.

The south porch is now the vestry, so entrance is through the north porch. Inside, the high quality of the restoration work is immediately apparent. On the walls each side of the slender tower arch hang the hatchments of the family, starting with that of the 6th Viscount Hereford (1677) through to the 3rd Marquis of Hertford (1842). The late twelfth-century font stands on a more recent base and is picturesquely described by Pevsner as 'a great stone cauldron'. The lovely eighteenth-century pulpit is exuberantly carved with foliage and cherubs and a family pew of the same period has panelling to match. On the north wall of the Gothic Revival style sanctuary is a large monument to Sir Michael Stanhope, privy councillor to both Elizabeth I and James I, who died in 1621. His undamaged, coloured alabaster figure, in full armour, kneels in profile. On a smaller scale, his widow, dressed in black, her hands struck off by iconoclasts, kneels in front of him and to his rear the bottom halves of two daughters, probably the work of the same iconoclastic excess. (Dowsing visited here in 1643. It is unclear if this is his work, although he did leave a very self-satisfied list of other damage he inflicted on this church.)

Once outside, note the very fine, bricked-up Norman doorway on the south wall. This caused a stir when it was uncovered during the Victorian restoration. Something that caused even more excitement was a chest that was discovered at about the same time, under the floor on the north side of the church. It contained 2,600 pennies dating mainly from the reign of Henry I, but also some from the reigns of Henry II, King John and William the Lion of Scotland.

ALL SAINTS SUDBOURNE

All Saints Sudbourne

ST MARY SWILLAND

St Mary Swilland

The nave and chancel

Some will love this extraordinary place; some will hate it; few will have nothing to say about it. It is a medley of styles and periods, including a Norman south doorway with traditional zig-zag arch and a Victorian nave joining what may have been part of a western tower built of sixteenth-century brick. The peculiar turret only adds to the overall fantasy. Designed in 1897 by J.S. Corder and described by Pevsner as 'an extraordinary contraption', it houses a fifteenth-century bell complete with a dormer window to project the sound.

If the exterior is fascinating, then the interior comes as a complete surprise. A Jacobean pulpit sits incongruously in a setting that looks more like a Russian Orthodox building than a Suffolk church. Indeed, for two hundred years this church housed a very valuable Russian icon until it was tragically stolen a few years ago. What appears to be a replica is now placed on the very ornate altar, but there is no information to be had on this strange Russian connection.

There is certainly nothing like this in Suffolk and I doubt if there is anything like it in the whole of England. Curiosity alone demands a visit to this puzzling building.

The altar

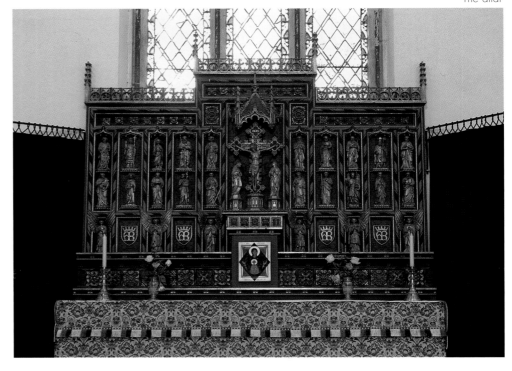

The tower and porch

Due to its proximity to some of the wilder parts of the east coast of Suffolk, this wonderfully picturesque round tower church has a host of stories of smugglers and excise men attached to it.

Set on high ground in a very pretty churchyard, the long nave and chancel is roofed with traditional reed thatch drained by wonderful animal gargoyles. This church is certainly Norman, but some experts claim that, because the walls are much thinner than one would expect of Norman builders, it is more likely Saxon in origin. In *c*.1300 the chancel was extended eastwards and the attractive octagonal belfry stage of the tower was constructed. An idea of the size of the earlier building can be got from the Norman corbel table below the eaves of the chancel. This stops half way along and clearly indicates where the original building ended. The porch and south aisle were added in *c*.1470. Among the many delights of this church are two impressive doors. The 500-year-old south door, with its beautifully carved tracery, opens into the church from the porch. Inside, the simple vestry door hides a superb Norman doorway with two orders of zig-zag mouldings on colonnades.

In 1917 a German zeppelin was brought down near by and most of the crew members were buried in the churchyard until their remains were removed to a German cemetery in the 1970s. Part of the crashed zeppelin is displayed in the porch.

The south colonnade

The nave

ST PETER THEBERTON

St Peter Theberton

ST MARY THORNHAM PARVA

This superb little church is well known both for its wall paintings and for its gorgeous mid-fourteenth-century painted retable, but the building itself is also a thing of simple beauty.

A picturesque and magically peaceful setting within a well kept churchyard accentuates the tranquillity of this building. The tower, chancel and nave are thatched in Norfolk reed and there are traces of Saxon flintwork in the largely Norman walls. A church has stood on this spot for well over a thousand years and the present building houses a treasure that one would be lucky to find in the great museums of the world.

On entering, loving restoration work stands side by side with the ancient. The wall paintings were very delicately restored in the 1980s and are of great interest; they depict the birth and early life of Christ on the south wall and, on the north wall, a rare sequence depicting the Martydom of St Edmund, complete with a wolf discovering the saint's severed head and Benedictine monks finally reburying the body. The whole interior is a joy, with its Georgian gallery, a fourteenth-century font decorated with simple tracery and some excellent medieval glass in the window of the south wall plus a chest (known as an 'ark') from the same period.

But the retable behind the altar is the crowning glory. It dates from the mid-fourteenth century, just prior to the Black Death, possibly from the royal workshops at Westminster, and is part of a much larger piece, originally in the Dominican Priory at Thetford in Norfolk. (The other half is thought to be a piece now in the Cluny Museum in Paris.) After the dissolution of the monasteries the retable was secretly kept in the private chapel of a Roman Catholic family in Stradbroke. It was rediscovered, undamaged, in the stable loft of Thornham Hall in 1927 and presented to the church by Lord Henniker. Breathtakingly beautiful, with its swaying figures, startling vitality and simply gorgeous design, this is a true gem and yet another ecclesiastical wonder of Suffolk.

The wall paintings

The retable

Wall painting depicting the Martyrdom of St Edmund

The rood screen

Troston is only seven miles from Bury St Edmunds, yet seems more remote, tucked picturesquely away down winding lanes. St Mary is known for its wall paintings, but is not as frequently visited as might be expected. The paintings are not all this building has to offer.

It is an old building and the exterior remains largely unchanged from its early plan. Mostly early thirteenth-century, with some fourteenth-century additions, it is, with the exception of the later Perpendicular porch, a fine example of the Early English style, the period which saw the first use of the pointed arch, as seen in the chancel, which is the earliest part of the church. The square, buttressed, corner tower was added in 1300, as evidenced by the tracery, which takes us into the early Decorated period. Next came the nave which, interestingly, until as late as 1869, was thatched along with chancel.

In the fifteenth century the ornate south porch was added, which, if not quite in keeping with the whole, makes its own statement. The flint and stone flushwork, famous throughout East Anglia, forms the basis of this addition, incorporating gargoyles and three vaulted, canopied niches that still retain the original pedestals, one with a supporting angel. They are, however, all missing their statues. Enter the church through a fourteenth-century arch, using the original 600-year-old door, which opens into a wide nave. Above there is a fine scissor-beamed roof, but the eye is immediately engaged by the paintings on the north wall of the nave: a large, still amazingly detailed, fourteenth-century St George slaying the dragon to the west and, to the east, a large St Christopher carrying the infant Jesus. Further to the west there are two more smaller paintings dated c.1250. One is a much earlier St George, the other a depiction of the Martyrdom of St Edmund (who was used as target practice by the Danes). There is also evidence of a doom painting above the chancel arch but the rood screen merely hints at its former glory.

There are many other delights in addition to the paintings, such as an interesting piscina set beneath thirteenth-century arches. This is a fairly rare example of a two-drain piscina, with one basin for the priest to wash his hands and a separate one to rinse the chalice. This dates it accurately to the reign of Edward I (1272–1307), the brief period when such examples occur. The fifteenth-century benches carry animal carvings and the lower half of a mermaid. There is also some rare medieval woodwork along the lower half of the east wall, some fourteenth-century stained glass and another piscina, this time with a cinquefoil arch, a fine sedilia and much more.

ST MARY TROSTON

St Mary Troston

ST MARY TUDDENHAM

St Mary Tuddenham

Not to be confused with the other Tuddenham near Ipswich, this is on the other side of Suffolk, near Mildenhall. Standing in a wild, overgrown churchyard full of tilting headstones, like a scene from *Wuthering Heights*, one might find it hard to believe that this is not an isolated spot and directly opposite the church are rows of modern houses. For no good reason this is a difficult church to get inside, but the exterior will repay those unlucky enough to have made a journey yet failed to get in. Mostly in the Decorated style, the lovely early fourteenth-century tower is striking, the front having two niches flanking a circular window with quatrefoil. The building obviously changed with the passing centuries, culminating in a general restoration in 1870.

Spend time walking round the outside, for there are pleasant surprises. If entry is possible, a hammerbeam roof, a part fourteenth-century font, a Jacobean pulpit and a very nice fourteenth-century piscina are among the things that come as a reward. As an extra bonus, look at the tomb recess, thought to be the resting place of Richard de Freville (died 1325) and then finish by admiring the four ancient doors, especially the lovely medieval linenfold vestry door.

ST MARY UGGLESHALL

From its entry in the Domesday Book, one would expect to find at least a substantial village at Uggleshall. Today, it lies down a rabbit warren of lanes, without even a signpost to help you locate it. People are few and far between, so asking is not an option and getting a little lost is almost mandatory. In the middle of nowhere this church keeps itself to itself.

In its timelessly bucolic setting, this is an unusual building with a Norman nave, a fourteenth-century chancel and a squat weatherboard tower stump that sits on a tower that was definitely under construction in the 1530s. What the tower originally looked like is hard to say, and some even claim the tower was never finished. Whatever used to crown it fell in the eighteenth-century to be replaced by what we see today. Indeed the church has had a history of collapsing parts. The entire east end was blown in during the 1987 storm but it has been tastefully rebuilt since then. The whole building, including the tower and charming little porch, is quaintly roofed with thatch. Evidence of the Norman pedigree of this church can be seen in the Norman arch of the blocked North door. Here we have a wonderful medley of styles, textures and materials that make this a must for anyone interested in church buildings.

St Mary Uggleshall

The Wenhaston Doom Painting

Before getting carried away about the well known treasure of Wenhaston, it should be noted that this is a lovely church in a beautiful setting and, although a little overshadowed by what is inside, it has much else to offer those prepared to look. Although the building is largely of Norman origin, the restoration work of 1892 that revealed the church's treasure also disclosed carved stones embedded in the east wall that suggest it might even be, in part, Saxon. The various periods are well represented by a fourteenth-century tower and an interesting nave, which was originally thatched and boasts two Norman windows. There is some Jacobean panelling and a Stuart pulpit. All this is accessed through a fifteenth-century porch with a very pretty doorway. Unfortunately, Dowsing and his thugs did a great deal of damage to this church in 1643. But various Victorian restoration programmes saved the building and, accidentally, but thankfully, revealed the treasure.

The Wenhaston Doom Painting, described by Pevsner (on what must surely have been a particularly grumpy day) as 'distressingly rustic' is quite simply remarkable. Painted in oil on wood panels between 1500 and 1520 it measures 17 × 8 feet and originally filled the upper part of the chancel arch as a background to a rood group. Covered in whitewash by the iconclasts and reused to hold the Royal Arms it was thrown out for burning during the 1892 restoration work. It rained that night, washing away some of the whitewash and revealing the beauty of what lay beneath. Cleaned and restored it is the most perfect painted tympanum to survive in this country. The colours are remarkably fresh and it is precisely that rustic simplicity that tells us so much about the times in which it was made, while still retaining its status as an object of great originality and beauty. One has only to look at the work of, say, Hieronymus Bosch or Bruegel to appreciate the true sophistication and symbolic depth of so many of these early religious pictorial statements. The idea that the State was destroying such imagery because it was poorly executed and primitive, serving only to mislead and terrify a simple-minded, ignorant and idolatrous congregation is unfounded. These acts of vandalism were simply political bullying and a yet another imposition by the State in its power struggle with the Church. All the roods in this country were destroyed on Cramer's orders in 1540; there are none left. The Wenhaston tympanum probably survived due to the fact that, unusually, it was actually attached to the rood. Orders were given that all roods were to be destroyed and replaced with Royal Coats of Arms, symbolising that the monarch was now in charge, not the Church. But why waste money destroying something that the Arms could be affixed to as the rood had been previously? Simply whitewash it over, reuse it and the job is done. For once an attempt at economy saved a priceless piece of religious history.

ST PETER WENHASTON

St Peter Wenhaston

ST PETRONILLA WHEPSTEAD

St Petronilla Whepstead

Nothing remains of the church on this site mentioned in the Domesday Book. What we see today is a pretty little building with a nave and chancel of the late thirteenth century and a late fifteenth-century tower. The tower once had a spire, which fell down in 1658, reputedly on the very night that Oliver Cromwell died. The original dedication of the church was to St Thomas of Canterbury, a dedication that reached cult status only to be stamped out in the 1530s and 1540s. The church was subsequently given the highly unusual dedication of St Petronilla, who is usually portrayed holding the keys of St Peter. An obscure Roman saint, she was, according to an implausible fifth-century legend, the daughter of St Peter. After her father heartlessly refused to cure her of paralysis, she recovered on her own and forgivingly spent the rest of her life serving him. This is the only such dedication in England.

A very interesting feature of the pleasant interior is the rood loft stair on the south wall. It is set deeply into a window bay. This is not unusual in itself, but the piscina drain cut into one of the steps is something that can be seen nowhere else.

What the church may lack in outstanding individual features is compensated for in the quiet beauty and calm that pervades it.

ALL SAINTS WORDWELL

All Saints Wordwell

This gorgeous little church, alas now redundant, is easily missed as one zooms past in the car. This is the parish of Culford, but there is no village to be seen beside this lonely little outpost on the edge of Elveden Forest. Prior to restoration in 1827, the church was completely dilapidated and being used as a granary. For once, it is the Victorians we have to thank for its preservation. What we see today we owe to the effort of one man, the famous church architect Samuel Saunders Teulon, who carried out his first, superbly sensitive restoration in 1857, followed by another, not quite so laudable, in 1866.

Predominantly Norman, and retaining an overall feeling of that period in its restored reincarnation, this lovely old building has a surprise to offer those who choose to stop and explore: the marvellous carvings, in both wood and stone, inside and outside. The first of these is encountered as one enters through Toulon's wooden porch. The Norman entrance doorway has a rare unrestored tympanum carved with a depiction of the Tree of Life. Two dogs howl at the base of the tree, their tails intertwining with the foliage. At the top of the right-hand doorjamb is a tiny man carved in stone with raised arms and, next to him, a peculiar carved symbol. On entering the church one meets him again, this time in a larger, far more primitive version on another tympanum that for some strange reason faces inwards over the blocked Norman north door. Here, there are two figures, one apparently holding a ring or a crown. The subject has become a matter of personal interpretation, but it is possible that this work is pagan, which would put the imagery and subject matter outside the realm of Christian iconography.

The carved wooden benches provide further wonderful flights of imagination and close to the door a bench back depicts dragons, rats, a jester and creatures with human heads all chasing one another. Who are they? What do they represent? We may never know for sure but personal speculation makes it all the more interesting.

ST MARY WORTHAM

St Mary Wortham

Carved bench ends

In the time of Edward the Confessor, Wortham was two parishes, each with its own church. After the Norman Conquest, there were still two parishes but what of the two churches? Could there have been a pre-Norman church on this site? Many think so and this is not hard to imagine.

Famously, the present church has the largest Norman round tower in Suffolk, a county that specialises in round towers: 62 feet high, 29 feet in diameter and built like a fortification, which some people believe it was. Local tradition tells of the tower having been there as a watchtower sometime before the present church but recent research has fairly comprehensively established that tower and nave were built at the same time, in 1160. The still formidable but truncated remains of the tower once housed four bells but in 1789 the roof and upper floors collapsed and the parish, probably still in shock, sold off the bells. In the eighteenth century a charming bellcote was added, its ogee top shyly peeping out from behind the once massive tower, perhaps as a faint apology for not rebuilding the original tower.

In style, the church is primarily Perpendicular but the south door of the chancel is distinctively of the Decorated period, as is the font. The aisles seem to have been added about 1360 with further work bringing the pretty clerestory in 1410. The stained glass windows, which added glory to this almost military structure were, apart form some small traces left in the shape of a cross in the east window, completely destroyed by Parliamentary Commission hooligans in 1653.

Inside is a pretty, but largely Victorian interior with a collection of very unusual and interesting bench ends; some old, and some re-carved in the nineteenth century by a local parishioner. The carvings include a tortoise, walrus and a striding Victorian journeyman, alongside quotes from Psalm 104. There are also memorials to the Betts family, who lived at the manor house for 425 years. An interesting story connects the manor house to the church. A secret door was found in the panelling of the library of the manor house. This led to a small room which may have been used to hide valuable church regalia during the Reformation and which still held unique local family records in the form of parchments and manuscripts going back to the year 1272.

This church is set next to very ancient common land and is has a distinct feel of England as it might have been at the time Norman Conquerors, standing strong and thick-set, with an air of absolute authority: a place of worship, which, in troubled times, could easily be adapted to a place of defence.

GLOSSARY

achievement of arms Heraldic arms in their fullest form, with a complete display of armorial motifs.

aisle The peripheral space usually running parallel with the nave; the chancel and transepts of a church may also be aisled.

alabaster A soft natural stone used for delicate carving. It is a granular form of gypsum, usually whitish-pink or yellowish in colour. It can be made nearly opaque by heating but the best is translucent white.

arcade A series of arches supported by pillars running down the sides of the nave of a church with aisles.

Arts and Crafts Movement A late nineteenth- to early twentieth-century movement opposing mass production and favouring hand crafted objects, taking its inspiration from the work of William Morris.

bay The area between two columns or piers of a row and including the wall and ceiling of the area, also applied to any area of wall surface divided by windows or a large vertical feature.

bellcote The framework on a roof from which the bells are hung.

bench ends The vertical section of the benches adjacent to an aisle, often richly carved with depictions of people, biblical scenes, grotesques and animals from nature or mythology.

boss A carved ornamentation at the intersection of roof beams or the ribs in vaulted ceilings, usually carrying representations of foliage, grotesque animals or figures.

box pews Large pews panelled to waist height or more, often with cushioned seats on three sides and sometimes even curtains. They are entered by a door from the aisle. Nicknamed box pews for their resemblance to horse boxes, they became popular in the seventeenth and early eighteenth century but in the restorations of the nineteenth century many disappeared.

brass An incised memorial made in an alloy called latten, bearing a portrait or inscription and usually found on the floor or on the top of tombs. The earliest brass in England is said to be dated 1277 (Sir John d'Abernon at Stoke Abernon in Surrey). Brasses were common until the first half of the seventeenth century, although there are some modern examples. The practice of taking rubbings has become very popular.

buttress A brickwork or masonry support projecting from (flying buttress) or built against a wall to give additional support.

cadaver tomb A tomb with a realistic and macabre representation of a corpse or skeleton.

canopy of honour A painted section of the roof of a church either over the altar or at the eastern end of the nave over the position occupied by the rood.

cenotaph tomb A sepulchral monument to someone buried elsewhere.

chancel The part of a church, including the altar and choir, reserved for the clergy. Sometimes separated from the nave by a rood screen.

cinquefoil see trefoil

clerestory An upper storey standing clear of its adjacent roofs and pierced by windows, the number of which usually corresponds to the number of bays in the arcade below.

collegiate-style seating Stalls that face each other rather than pews facing forwards.

corbel A block of stone projecting from a wall, supporting some horizontal feature. Often carved or moulded.

corbel table Row of exterior or interior corbels supporting a roof, parapet or cornice and usually connected. A feature of Norman buildings.

crocketed Small projecting sculptural feature in the form of leaves or flowers, used on pinnacles, spires, canopies, etc., first appearing in the Decorated period in the first half of fourteenth century, carried through to the later Perpendicular style.

cupola Small polygonal or circular domed turret crowning a roof.

dado Decorative covering of lower part of a wall.

Decorated Style of English Gothic architecture covering the period from 1290 to 1350.

doom painting A depiction of the Last Judgment, normally found painted over the chancel arch (which symbolically separated earthly from heavenly things). Christ is typically represented sitting on a rainbow with souls being weighed below before being sent to join the blessed on his right hand side or the damned on his left.

family pew Seats set aside for the use of a local family.

fan vault The ultimate development of English Gothic vaulting of the Perpendicular period. It takes the form of trumpet-shaped, inverted semi-cones of masonry in fan-like shapes enriched by tracery springing in equal proportions in all directions.

fleurons Decorative carved flowers or leaves.

flushwork The decorative use of flint in conjunction with dressed stone to form patterns, tracery and sometimes lettering and initials.

fluting Vertical channelling in the shaft of a column.

font A structure designed to hold the holy water that is used at baptism. Most are made of stone but a few lead ones survive.

gargoyles Water spouts projecting from the parapet of a wall or tower to throw rain water clear. They are carved mainly in the form of grotesques, animal and monsters.

Gothic Period of architecture from the twelfth to the fifteenth century and embodied in the Early English and Decorated styles. The original influence was the architecture of twelfth-century France.

Gothic Revival Serious but not always successful, project by early nineteenth-century designers and architects to build in the true Gothic style.

grotesques Fanciful and often frightening decorations, combining men and animals into strange creatures.

hammerbeam Projecting right-angled beam or bracket, shaped like a hammer at the foot of the curved member or principal rafter in a wooden roof. Often decorated and supporting vertical or arched braces.

hatchment Diamond-shaped memorial painting depicting the arms or family crest of the deceased against a background that shows their sex and marital status. These boards were carried in procession at the burial of the holder of the arms. For some months after they were kept at the deceased's house then finally transferred to the church walls.

herringbone A pattern formed in masonry by a zig-zag of diagonally placed stones alternatively inclining to left and right.

king post An upright roof beam set between horizontal cross beams or between cross beam and roof ridge, to prevent sag and give greater stability.

Lady Chapel Chapel dedicated to the Virgin Mary, usually to the east of the main altar in a large church.

lancet Tall narrow light which is sharply pointed at the top and a feature of early English architecture. Often found in groups of three and five, groups of seven are known but far less common.

linenfold Series of wooden panels, carved to look like pieces of material hanging vertically in natural folds.

lychgate Covered entrance to the churchyard. Originally provided cover for shrouded bodies and later a resting place for the coffin to await the priest.

minstrel gallery Upper storey above an aisle or at the west end of the nave. The area was used by small village bands during the seventeenth, eighteenth and early nineteenth centuries.

misericord A carved bracket supporting a hinged seat when it is turned up for use. Often beautifully carved and ornamented with both ecclesiastical subjects as well as more grotesque and eccentric themes.

mullion Vertical post or upright dividing a window into two or more lights.

multifoil see trefoil

nave The area between the chancel and the west end, in which the congregation is housed during services.

niche Vertical hollow or ornamental recess in a wall, designed to hold a small statue.

Norman English building style from 1066–1200. Impressive massive buildings with a large variety of mouldings on arches and doorways, semi-circular arches, barrel vaults and mostly square towers. Aisles were a later addition of the period.

ogee A continuous flowing S-shaped arch or moulding. A convex curve flows into a concave one. They are not usually very large since the design is not capable of bearing heavy loads, but their elegance adorns the heads of canopies over piscina, sedilia and other delicate traceries.

paraclose screen The partition or screen around a shrine, chapel or tomb, in order to separate it from the main body of the church.

pedestal Supporting base between a column and the plinth.

Perpendicular Style running from about 1350–1539, a period when church building achieved its ultimate splendour with lofty proportions, vertical lines, huge windows, high arches, traceried panels and elaborate decoration, battlemented parapets and flying buttresses. Much of this was made possible by the wealth of wool merchants.

pews Wooden bench seats often enclosed by high walls with doors.

piscina Niche containing a stone bowl or drain. Usually built into a wall of the chancel near an altar. Sometimes built under an elaborate canopy. Used for washing sacred vessels the water drained to consecrated ground outside the church walls.

poppyhead A floral or leaf-like carving decorating a bench or choir stall.

Pre-Raphaelite Brotherhood Established in 1848, a group of Victorian artists who sought to return to the principles that were followed before Raphael (died 1520) imposed his mark.

They included Rossetti, Millais and Holman Hunt. Their preoccupation with biblical and literary subjects led to a revival by William Morris and Burne-Jones, which left its impression on English stained glass of the period.

pulpit Raised platform from which the preacher delivers his sermon. Most are carved in wood but there are a few rare stone ones.

quatrefoil see trefoil

rederos Decorated screen or wall-covering behind an altar beneath the east window. Can be tapestry, painting or a stone construction shaped to show the twelve apostles.

retable Raised shelf behind altar, used to hold ornaments such as candlesticks, etc.

rood beam Horizontal beam spanning the chancel and sometimes the aisles supports a representation of a crucifix (rood).

rood loft Gallery on top of the rood screen usually carved and containing a large cross, sometimes with a rood group, consisting of the crucified Christ, St John and the Virgin. It was reached using the rood stairs often cut into, or through a pillar. Many were destroyed at the time of the Reformation.

rood screen A wooden or stone screen dividing the nave from choir and chancel, often elaborately carved and painted.

sanctuary Area to the east of the altar rails all around and including the altar.

sanctuary ring Door knocker on the exterior door of a church. It was used by persons wishing to claim the ancient right of sanctuary within the church or churchyard, until such time as they could be lawfully brought to trial.

sanctus bell Small bell hung, usually in its own turret, on the exterior of the church at the junction of the nave and chancel. The bell is rung at the elevation of the host.

Saxon Period covering roughly 600–1066. The churches built at this time were simple, single or two-cell buildings with a western entrance often in wood but later in stone. Many round towers are of Saxon origin with later churches added.

scissor-beam A roof in which the beams are crossed and interlocked diagonally in the shape of an open pair of scissors.

scratch dial A circle incised in the stone on or near the doorway of many old churches. It is usually about six inches across with lines radiating from a centre hole into which a peg was inserted to make a primitive sundial used to tell the times for masses.

sedilia Set of three or four seats, recessed in niches in the south wall of the chancel, used by the priest and his assistants. Often set under decorative canopied arches.

septaria A local Suffolk stone found on the cliffs and beaches.

seven sacrament font A type of fifteenth- and sixteenth-century octagonal font, almost exclusive to East Anglia, on which are carved illustrations of Baptism, Confirmation, Mass, Matrimony, Penance, Ordination to Priesthood and Extreme Unction. The eighth panel sometimes shows the baptism of Christ. Many of these fonts were mutilated by iconoclasts.

sounding board Horizontal canopy above the pulpit helping to carry the preacher's voice by deflection of sound.

spandrel The space between two arches, also the triangle-shaped blocking between the posts and beams of screens or roofs.

spire Tall conical structure tapering to a point, often topped with a weather vane, and built on top of a tower. Differs from a steeple in that it can be seen as a separate appendage to the tower; a steeple is an integral part of it.

squint A hole made in a wall or pillar between aisle and chancel through which the main altar can be viewed. Sometimes known as a hagloscope.

table tomb Masonry tomb in the shape of an altar.

three-decker pulpit A pulpit in three ascending tiers, one each for the clerk, the reader and the preacher. Due to the height of seventeenth- and eighteenth-century box pews the preacher had to be especially high up if the congregation were to be able to see and hear him.

tie beam Enormous horizontal main beam in a timber roof, spanning the distance between two walls and acting as a truss supporting the roof.

tracery Ornamental work in wood or stone in a window screen or panelling.

transepts Arms projecting from the point where nave and chancel meet in a traditional cruciform church.

transoms The horizontal crosspieces in window tracery, mostly seen in Perpendicular style windows.

trefoil From the twelfth century, foils were a much used decoration in Gothic churches. The Early English style produced the trefoiled (three leafed shape), intended to represent the Trinity. This was followed by the quatrefoil (four leafed) the cinquefoil (five leafed) and the multifoil.

tympanum Space between the lintel of a doorway and the arch above.

Vanitas Moralia A sculpture or image representing the transient quality of earthly existence and the vanity of man. Usually depicts a skeleton or cadaver.

vault Arched roof, ceiling or arch-like structures with ribs radiating from one central point.

wagon roof Curved roof with similarly shaped rafters resembling the interior of a covered wagon.

wall plates Horizontal pieces of timber placed on top of either side of walls into support the load of the rafters in the roof above.

FURTHER READING

Bottomly, Frank, *The Explorer's Guide to the Abbeys, Monasteries and Churches of Great Britain* (Avenel, New York, 1984)

Cox, Charles J., *The Parish Churches of England* (B.T. Batsford, London, 1954)

Jenkins, Simon, *England's Thousand Best Churches* (Penguin, London, 1999)

Jones, Lawrence E., *The Beauty of English Churches* (Constable, London, 1978)

Mortlock, D.P., *The Popular Guide to Suffolk Churches* No. 1 West Suffolk, No. 2 Central Suffolk, No. 3 East Suffolk (Acorn, Cambridge, 1992)

Pevsner, Nikolaus, *The Buildings of England: Suffolk* (Penguin, London, 1961)

www.suffolkchurches.co.uk
www.syllysuffolk.co.uk
www.williamdowsing.org

All the photographs in this book may be ordered direct from David Stanford.

Visit www.suffolkchurches.net for details